Better Homes and Gardens®

CHRISTMAS

FROM THE HEART®

Volume 19

Meredith® Consumer Marketing
Des Moines, Iowa

Better Homes and Gardens®

CHRISTMAS
FROM THE HEART®

Meredith Corporation Consumer Marketing
Senior Vice President, Consumer Marketing: David Ball
Consumer Product Marketing Director: Steve Swanson
Consumer Product Marketing Manager: Wendy Merical
Business Director: Ron Clingman
Associate Director, Production: Douglas M. Johnston
Photographers: Marty Baldwin, Scott Little,
Kritsada Panichgul, Jay Wilde

Waterbury Publications, Inc.
Contributing Editor: Carol Field Dahlstrom
Contributing Graphic Designer: Angie Haupert Hoogensen
Editorial Director: Lisa Kingsley
Associate Editor: Tricia Laning
Creative Director: Ken Carlson
Associate Design Director: Doug Samuelson
Production Assistants: Kim Hopkins, Mindy Samuelson
Contributing Food Editor: Lois White
Contributing Food Stylist: Charles Worthington
Contributing Copy Editor: Terri Fredrickson
Contributing Proofreaders: Gretchen Kauffman, Margaret Smith

Better Homes and Gardens® Magazine
Editor in Chief: Gayle Goodson Butler
Art Director: Michael D. Belknap
Deputy Editor, Food and Entertaining: Nancy Wall Hopkins
Senior Food Editor: Richard Swearinger
Associate Food Editor: Erin Simpson
Editorial Assistant: Renee Irey

Meredith Publishing Group
President: Jack Griffin
Executive Vice President: Andy Sareyan
Vice President, Manufacturing: Bruce Heston

Meredith Corporation
Chairman of the Board: William T. Kerr
President and Chief Executive Officer: Stephen M. Lacy

In Memoriam: E.T. Meredith III (1933–2003)

All of us at Meredith Consumer Marketing are dedicated to pro-
viding you with information and ideas to enhance your home.
We welcome your comments and suggestions. Write to us at:
Meredith Consumer Marketing, 1716 Locust St.,
Des Moines, IA 50309-3023.

Better Homes and Gardens®
CHRISTMAS
FROM THE HEART®

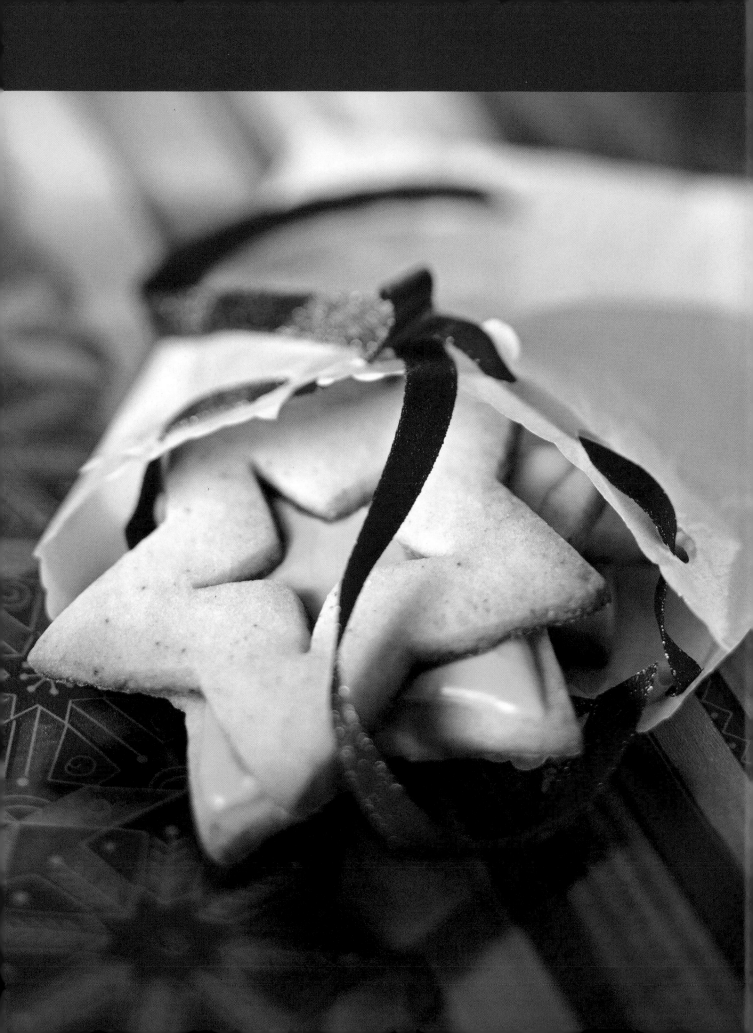

contents

*Every corner of your holiday home
will sparkle and shine with handmade trims
you make yourself.*

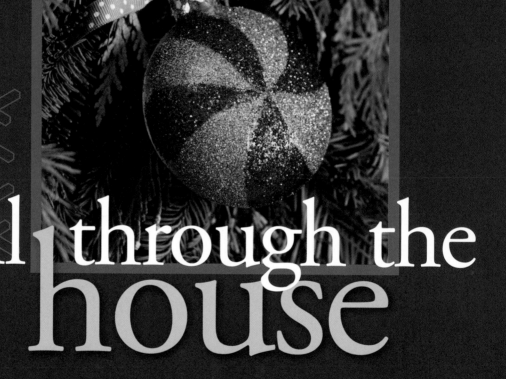

all through the
house

Make your banister sugarplum sweet with an array of dreamy projects.

Clear glass ornaments are painted with glue and dusted with glitter to make

Swirled Glittery Trims, *above*, adding the perfect touch of Christmas

sparkle. Tie on some **Fleecy Faux Candies** in sugary pastel colors and

Sweet Lollipop Treats made from purchased candies. Turn the page to

see the ornaments and trims that make this banister a dream come true.

Create toddler-safe **Fleecy Faux Candies**, *left*, using inexpensive fleece and pretty ribbons. Everyone will reach for **Sweet Lollipop Treats**, *below left*, that you present on your sugarplum banister. Purchased lollipops are simply wrapped in cellophane and tied with a wide ribbon.

Toss-away sweaters become **Old-Fashioned Sweater Stockings**, *opposite*, to hold the dearest gifts. The simple pattern can be adapted many ways. Fill these warm stockings with candy, tuck in small gifts, or surprise someone with a sweet little kitten to love. For patterns and instructions, see pages 18–19.

Choose rich wool fabric to make a **Pretty Poinsettia Pillow**, *above*. The poinsettia shapes are layered for a realistic look, and blanket stitching adds texture to this elegant pillow.

Adorn your holiday table with an heirloom-quality **Quilted Holly Table Runner**, *opposite*. The appliqué holly center is set off with pieced borders and softly scalloped edges. For patterns and instructions, see pages 20–21.

Keep it simple yet elegant by setting your holiday table in a monochromatic color scheme of natural green and white. Clear candlesticks in varying styles hold shades of green tapers as they surround a **Naturally Green Centerpiece**, *opposite* and *below*. The centerpiece rests beautifully on a footed cake plate. To complete the table, make **Partridge in a Pear Name Cards**, *above*. Each name is written on a cardstock paper partridge that rests in a real Bosc pear. For instructions and patterns, see page 22.

Every day is special when you gather around the **Family Advent Calendar**, *opposite,* to share a small gift. This clever calendar is made using a place mat and colorful rickrack.

The message says it all when you stitch the **Home Is Where the Heart Is Cross-Stitch Sampler**, *above.* Taken from a vintage pattern, this piece is worked over 3 threads and uses only basic cross-stitches. For patterns and instructions, see page 23.

Decorate your homespun Christmas tree with soft and simple handmade ornaments in red and white. The **Felted Mitten Trims,** *above left* and *below right*, are created using a clever cut-out technique and feature favorite holiday motifs. The **Candy Cane Yarn Balls,** *above right*, wind pretty yarns together for a candy-stripe appearance. For instructions see pages 24–25.

Swirled Glittery Trims
Shown on page 6

WHAT YOU NEED
Clear glass flat round ornaments
    (available at crafts stores)
Fine line marker
Crafts glue
Paintbrush
Fine pink glitter in two shades
8-inch length of polka-dot ribbon

WHAT YOU DO
Be sure the ornament is clean and dry.
Using the fine line marker, draw swirls
on the front of the ornament, making
8 sections. Draw the sections as evenly
as possible, but they do not have to be
exact. Use a paintbrush to brush glue on
every other section of the marked swirls.
Sprinkle with glitter. Let dry. Repeat for
the other sections using a darker shade
of pink glitter. Add a polka-dot ribbon
for hanging.

Fleecy Faux Candies
Shown on pages 7–8

WHAT YOU NEED
¼ yard of pink fleece
¼ yard of white fleece fabric
Clear cellophane
Scissors
Transparent tape
Narrow ribbon in two colors of pink

WHAT YOU DO
1. For each faux candy, cut 2 strips of
pink and 2 strips of white fleece that are
each 1×18 inches long. Layer the fleece

on top of each other with two pink strips
together and 2 white strips together.
2. Roll up the layered strips and lay
them on a piece of cellophane cut to
7×9 inches. Roll the cellophane around
the rolled fleece and secure with tape.
3. Use two colors of ribbon to tie the
ends close to the rolled fleece. Trim the
cellophane ends to desired length. Use
one of the ribbons for hanging.

Sweet Lollipop Treats
Shown on pages 7–8

WHAT YOU NEED
Purchased lollipops
Cellophane
Wide ribbon
Pinking shears
10-inch length of narrow ribbon

WHAT YOU DO
Remove the lollipop from the original
wrapping, leaving the tightly wrapped
plastic on the candy if available, or wrap
with cellophane if necessary. Cut a
6-inch piece of ribbon and tie at the base
of the candy. Tie another knot; trim ends
with pinking shears. Tie the narrow ribbon
at the base of the lollipop for hanging.

Old-Fashioned Sweater
Stockings
Shown on page 9

WHAT YOU NEED
Tracing paper or copier; pencil
Old sweaters to cut up
Matching thread; scissors
¼ yard cotton fabric for lining
Trims, such as buttons, tassels, and
    embroidery thread

WHAT YOU DO
1. Enlarge and trace or copy patterns,
opposite. Place sweater pieces right sides
together and cut 2 of the stocking
patterns from each of the sweater fabrics
and cotton lining fabrics. From sweater
fabric, cut a 2×7-inch strip for the
hanging loop and a 12×6-inch piece
for the cuff.
2. With right sides together, stitch
around side edges of the stocking and
lining pieces, leaving top edges open.
Use a ¼-inch seam allowance for the
linings and a ⅜-inch seam allowance
for the sweater fabrics. (Because the
sweater fabrics are so stretchy when cut,
it is helpful to sew seams using an even
feed foot on the sewing machine,

**OLD-FASHIONED
SWEATER STOCKING POCKET**
Enlarge 200%
Cut 1

OLD-FASHIONED SWEATER STOCKING
Enlarge 200%
Cut 2, reversing 1

reduce pressure on the presser foot, and lengthen the stitch to help the stocking keep its shape.)

3. Clip curves and turn sweater stocking pieces right side out. Insert lining inside stocking sweater piece, with wrong sides together and top edges even.

4. With right sides together, sew long edge of loop piece together. Turn right side out. With right sides together, sew short side of cuff piece to form a tube. Place hanging loop down inside stocking at side edge; overlap raw edges of ends at top edge of stocking. Baste through all layers of stocking, lining, and loop. Insert cuff inside stocking, with right side of cuff against the right side of the stocking lining. Sew around top edge through all layers, using a ⅜-inch seam allowance.

5. Flip cuff piece out over front of stocking, rolling cut edge underneath to form a 3½-inch-wide finished cuff on the outside. Using thread to match the cuff, tack the cuff to the stocking by sewing a few stitches through both layers at the side seams.

6. To add details to stockings:
For patches and pocket, trace or copy patterns, *above* and *below.* Press back with iron-on interfacing. Hand stitch to stocking. *For buttons,* sew buttons to top of stocking at cuff. *For tassel,* attach tassel to zipper pull.

**OLD-FASHIONED
SWEATER
STOCKING
HEEL**
Enlarge 200%
Cut 1

**OLD-FASHIONED
SWEATER
STOCKING
TOE**
Enlarge 200%
Cut 1

19

Pretty Poinsettia Pillow
Shown on page 10

WHAT YOU NEED
13-inch square ivory-color felted wool
Scraps of red and green felted wool
13-inch square of printed flannel for
    backing
Matching sewing thread
Ivory perle cotton
12 size 6/0 gold color glass seed beads
12-inch pillow form
Tracing paper and pencil

WHAT YOU DO
1. Enlarge and trace or copy the three flower patterns and one leaf pattern, *below.* Cut three flower shapes from scraps of red felted wool and six leaf shapes from green felted wool scraps. Find center of ivory wool and lay largest red flower piece onto center. Center medium-size red flower wool piece onto first flower shape. Add smallest flower piece on top of other two and pin in place. Position green wool leaves underneath flower shapes and pin in place.
2. With a single strand of sewing thread, baste shapes in place onto ivory wool. Using a single strand of ivory perle cotton, stitch shapes onto backing fabric using blanket stitch. Sew beads to center of top flower shape.
3. Trim front and back fabric pieces to 12½-inch-square size. With right sides together stitch pillow front to back, using ½-inch seam allowance, leaving an opening for stuffing. Clip corners and turn pillow right side out. Insert pillow form and slipstitch opening closed.

Quilted Holly Table Runner
Shown on page 11

WHAT YOU NEED
Fabrics shown are from the "I Believe in Santa" 100% cotton fabrics by Nancy Halversen.

Finished size: Approx. 20×38 inches

Scraps of green for leaves
Scraps of red for berries
Scraps of lighter green for holly vine;
    make 30 inches of ¼-inch finished
    bias strip
8×26-inch light blue piece for center
    background
Five 3½-inch squares of four different
    fabrics for first border
Four 3½-inch squares of one fabric for
    first border
½ yard stripe fabric for outside border;
    cut into three 6-inch strips
4¼ yards of ⅛-inch-wide cording or
    drapery cording for piping
¼ yard teal fabric for piping, cut across
    width to make five 1-inch strips
½ yard teal fabric for bias binding
    around outside edges; cut
    into 2-inch bias strips to make
    approximately 130 inches of double-
    fold bias binding

PRETTY
POINSETTIA PILLOW
LEAF
Enlarge 200%
Cut 6

PRETTY
POINSETTIA PILLOW
MEDIUM FLOWER
Enlarge 200%
Cut 1

PRETTY
POINSETTIA PILLOW
LARGE FLOWER
Enlarge 200%
Cut 1

PRETTY
POINSETTIA PILLOW
SMALL FLOWER
Enlarge 200%
Cut 1

⅝ yard of fabric for backing; cut to
    22×40-inch piece
22×40-inch piece of thin cotton batting
Matching sewing threads
Quilting thread
Appliqué patterns; marking pen
Tracing paper
Green embroidery thread and needle

WHAT YOU DO

1. Enlarge if necessary and trace or copy patterns, *right* and *below*. Make bias strips for ¼-inch holly vine and appliqué in place onto light blue center fabric. Appliqué green holly leaves onto center fabric. Using three strands green embroidery floss sew stem outline stitch along center vein lines of holly leaves. Appliqué red berries over leaves and vine. Trim center piece to measure 6½×24½ inches.
2. Make piping by covering narrow cording with teal fabric strips and stitching close to cording. Use ¼-inch seam allowances for all seams. Stitch piping in place around center appliqué piece by stitching long sides first and then the ends. Sew 3½-inch squares together and sew to center piece. Add piping

around ouer edge of pieced border. Piece together striped outside border fabric to make two 39-inch strips and two 23-inch strips. Sew strips to outside edges of first border, mitering corners.
3. Layer backing, batting, and pieced top; quilt as desired. Trace outside scallop

border pattern to tracing paper. Lay pattern over outside borders, making sure corners come together at the miter. Pin in place and cut around outside edges. Make bias binding and attach to outside edges.

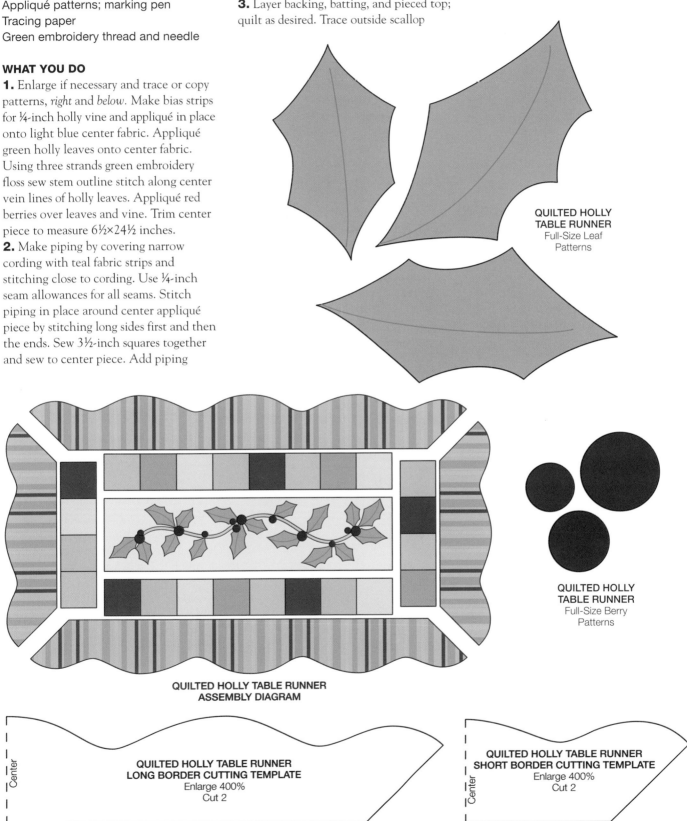

**QUILTED HOLLY
TABLE RUNNER**
Full-Size Leaf
Patterns

**QUILTED HOLLY
TABLE RUNNER**
Full-Size Berry
Patterns

**QUILTED HOLLY TABLE RUNNER
ASSEMBLY DIAGRAM**

**QUILTED HOLLY TABLE RUNNER
LONG BORDER CUTTING TEMPLATE**
Enlarge 400%
Cut 2

Center

**QUILTED HOLLY TABLE RUNNER
SHORT BORDER CUTTING TEMPLATE**
Enlarge 400%
Cut 2

Center

Naturally Green Centerpiece

Shown on pages 12–13

WHAT YOU NEED

Clear glass compote or cake plate
Fresh fruits and vegetables such as
    green grapes, artichokes, and pears
Fresh greens

WHAT YOU DO

Arrange the fruit on the plate or
compote. Tuck greens under and around
the fruits and vegetables.

Partridge in a Pear Name Cards

Shown on pages 12–13

WHAT YOU NEED

Tracing paper; pencil
Small piece of cream-color cardstock
Scissors
Crafts glue

Gold marking pen; knife
Fresh pear
Narrow ribbon

WHAT YOU DO

Trace or copy the partridge patterns,
below. Trace patterns onto the cardstock
and cut out. Fold the wings as indicated
and glue to each side of bird body. Let
dry. Write the name of the guest on the
bird body using the gold marking pen.
Cut a slit into the pear. Slide the bird
into the slit. Set on a plate and tie
a ribbon around the stem of the pear.

Family Advent Calendar

Shown on page 14

WHAT YOU NEED

14×19-inch red place mat
Tracing paper, marking pencil
Assorted scraps of plain and printed
    cotton fabric in lime green, kelly
    green, pink, and red
2 3×20-inch strips stripe cotton fabric
¼ yard heavyweight iron-on interfacing
Scraps of red, lime green, dark green,
    and pink felted wool
50 inches *each* of green, lime green,
    and pink ⅜-inch-wide rickrack

1 sheet heavy-weight lime green
    decorative paper for numbers
Matching sewing threads
Fabric glue
Holly leaf stickers (found in
    scrapbooking sections)
13½-inch length of ⅜-inch dowel stick

WHAT YOU DO

1. Trace or copy circle pattern, *opposite
below*, onto paper and cut out. Cut out
twenty-four 2½×3-inch rectangles from

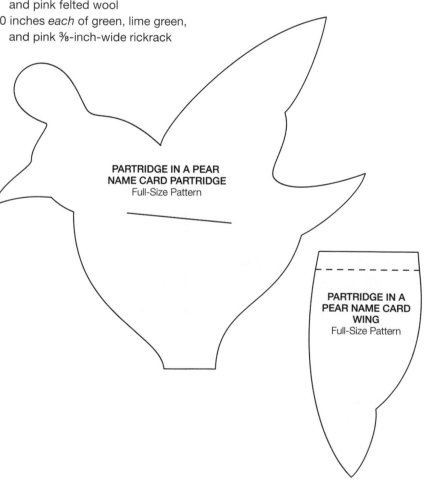

**PARTRIDGE IN A PEAR
NAME CARD PARTRIDGE**
Full-Size Pattern

**PARTRIDGE IN A
PEAR NAME CARD
WING**
Full-Size Pattern

assorted cotton fabrics. Cut out twenty-four 2×2½-inch pieces of interfacing. Cut out 24 circles from assorted colors of wool felt. Cut numbers from decorative paper using die-cut machine found in scrapbooking stores. Fuse interfacing to back sides of fabric pieces. Fold ¼ inch around all sides of fabric pieces and iron to the back. Stitch close to folded edge along one long side for the top hem. Place circles in center of fabric pieces and machine stitch in place using blanket stitch around circle edges.

2. Place fabric pockets evenly on top of place mat, leaving 1 inch around all side edges. Pin in place. Slip rickrack underneath side and lower edges and stitch pockets to place mat, stitching close to folded edges of fabric pieces. Glue numbers in place over wool circles. Glue holly motifs at topside edges, center, and lower edge.

3. To make striped bow hanger, fold each long strip of fabric, right sides together. Angle cut one end of each strip. Stitch along long edge and end angle cut, using ¼-inch seam allowance. Turn right side out and press. Tack fabric cut ends to back of place mat by hand stitching in place at side edges. Place dowel stick at the back top edge of placemat, over the fabric bow ends. Tack in place by stitching by hand over dowel stick and through a few threads of the back of the place mat. Tie fabric lengths into a bow at the center.

Home Is Where the Heart Is Cross-Stitch Sampler

Shown on page 15

WHAT YOU NEED
8×10-inch piece of 30-count
  evenweave fabric
Cotton embroidery floss in colors listed
  in key, *right*

FAMILY
ADVENT CALENDAR
Full-Size Pattern

Cross-stitch needle
Embroidery hoop
Scissors
Iron

WHAT YOU DO
Find the center of the chart and the center of the fabric. Begin stitching there. Use 2 plies of floss for all cross-stitches, working over 3 strands of fabric. Press piece on back side. Frame as desired.

1 Square = 1 Stitch

COLOR KEY

■ 310 Black |I| 553 Medium violet   ✚ 725 Topaz   − 3806 Pink
▲ 321 Christmas red |O| 563 Seafoam   ✕ 3766 Peacock blue   # 3828 Tan

Felted Mitten Trims
Shown on page 16

WHAT YOU NEED

2 5×6-inch pieces of felt for each
   mitten
1 4×6-inch piece of contrasting
   color felt for chosen design
   and cuff
Tracing paper

**FELTED MITTEN
TRIMS**
Full-Size Patterns

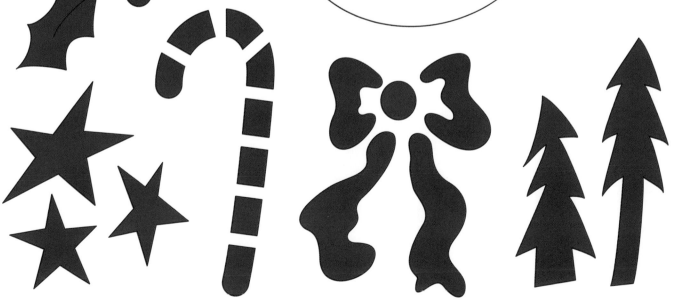

Marking pencil
Sewing thread to match mitten
  color
Sharp, pointed small sewing
  scissors
Fabric glue
Pinking shears

WHAT YOU DO

1. Trace or copy the mitten, cuff, and desired motif patterns, *opposite*, onto tracing paper and cut out. Cut 2 mitten body pieces from felt and cut 1 cuff from contrasting felt color. Straight or pinking shears may be used to vary the looks. Mitten cuff may be fringed at the bottom by making small cuts up from the bottom edge or by cutting small holes at lower edge for a lacey look.

2. For the chosen motif design, cut a slightly larger square from contrasting felt. For the hanging loop, cut a 5×⅜-inch strip of felt. Trace desired pattern onto paper and cut out about ¼ inch around outside edges. Place contrasting color of felt square on back side of mitten front at desired location.

3. Place pattern on top felt square. Working from the back side of the mitten and using sewing thread matching the mitten body, straight stitch around motif lines. Using a darning foot and stitching free motion with the sewing machine makes small adjustments in stitching easier. Turn mitten to front and carefully clip away felt inside and very close to

sewing stitches, being careful to cut away only the top layer of felt to reveal the contrasting felt design.

4. On the back side, trim away extra felt around outside edge of design. Fold loop in half and place at top side edge of mitten inside back. Stitch across bottom cut edges through mitten back. Place mitten front on top of mitten back and straight stitch close to side and lower edges. Glue cuff at top edge of mitten.

Candy Cane Yarn Balls
Shown on page 16

WHAT YOU NEED

3-inch-diameter foam ball, such as
  Styrofoam
Red and white cotton yarn
Crafts glue
Straight pins
Wet washcloth in a dish
Tumbler

WHAT YOU DO

1. Pull a length of yarn from both colors and hold them together. You will be wrapping the ball with the two yarns together. Start at the middle of the foam ball and pin the yarns in place. See Photo A.

2. Make lines of glue on the foam ball and begin wrapping the yarns around the foam ball. *Note:* Frequently wipe fingers on the wet washcloth to keep them from

getting sticky and pulling the yarn back off. Use pins to hold yarn in place if needed. Continue to wrap until one side is completed. See Photo B.

3. Make a loop with the yarn and glue and pin in place for hanging. See Photo C. Note: Use a tumbler to hold the ball while working if desired.

4. Repeat wrapping on the other side without adding the loop. Let dry. Remove unnecessary pins.

*Create irresistible goodies
and craft simple, stylish packaging that will
merit admiring "oohs" and "aahs."*

sweet gifts
from the kitchen

Tempting treats, such as **Festive Sandwich Stars**, *above*, and

Caramel-Hazelnut Brownies, *opposite,* are welcome gifts for loved

ones. Package cookies in parchment paper bags and brownies in

colorful boxes embellished with ribbon. Recipes are on page 33.

Dress up boxes, containers, or vinyl bags with festive papers and trims to hold **White and Dark Chocolate Chunk Cookies,** *above left,* **Fruit Dream Cookies,** *above right,* and **Cardamom Snowman Cutouts,** *right.* Present **Peppermint Palmiers,** *opposite,* on an elegant platter. Recipes are on pages 34–35.

With a bit of creativity and a few eye-catching embellishments, transform plain-as-can-be **Santa Cutouts**, *above left,* into festive works of art. Holiday-green pistachios and ribbon wrap **Crisp Mini Biscotti**, *above right,* as stunning packages. Recipes are on pages 35–36.

Share a heartfelt message. Tie an evergreen sprig and handmade gift card to a bottle of **Holiday Cranberry Syrup**, *above left.* Line several boxes with fancy papers to hold scrumptious **Lemon Curd Bars**, *above right.* One batch makes 32 bars. Recipes are on page 36.

Spiff up an old breadboard with ribbon and use it to hold **Cranberry-Orange Loaf**, *right.* Delight party hosts with an assortment of **Little Pumpkin Cakes with Nut Brittle Shards,** *below.* Recipes are on page 37.

Festive Sandwich Stars

You'll need two sizes of cutters to make these cookies. Shown on page 26.

WHAT YOU NEED

- ⅔ cup butter, softened
- ¾ cup granulated sugar
- 1 teaspoon baking powder
- ¼ teaspoon salt
- 1 egg
- 1 tablespoon milk
- 2 teaspoons vanilla
- 2 cups all-purpose flour
- 1 tablespoon butter
- 2 cups powdered sugar
  Green and/or red food coloring

WHAT YOU DO

1. Preheat oven to 375°F. In a medium mixing bowl beat ⅔ cup butter with an electric mixer on medium to high speed for 30 seconds. Add granulated sugar, baking powder, and salt. Beat until combined, scraping sides of bowl occasionally. Beat in egg, milk, and

1 teaspoon of the vanilla until combined. Beat in as much flour as you can with the mixer. Using a wooden spoon, stir in any remaining flour. Divide dough in half.

2. On a lightly floured surface roll half of the dough at a time to ⅛-inch thickness. Using a 2½-inch star-shape cutter, cut out dough. Using a smaller star-shape cutter, cut out centers of half the cookies. Place cutouts 1 inch apart on ungreased cookie sheets.

3. Bake for 7 to 8 minutes or until edges are firm. Transfer to wire racks; cool. Repeat with remaining dough, rerolling dough scraps.

4. For filling, in a bowl beat 1 tablespoon butter with an electric mixer on medium speed for 30 seconds. Beat in remaining 1 teaspoon vanilla and the powdered sugar until combined. If necessary, beat in milk, 1 teaspoon at a time, to make an icing of soft spreading consistency. Tint icing with green and/or red food coloring.

5. Spread icing on the flat sides (bottoms) of the cookies without cutout centers. Top with remaining cookies, flat sides down, offsetting points. Makes about 18 cookie sandwiches.

To Store: Layer cookies between sheets of waxed paper in an airtight container; cover. Store in the refrigerator up to 3 days or freeze up to 3 months.

Caramel-Hazelnut Brownies

These dreamy brownies feature three luscious layers: fudgy brownie, hazelnut-flecked caramel, and an intensely flavored dark chocolate topping. Shown on page 27.

WHAT YOU NEED

- 3 cups all-purpose flour
- 1½ cups unsweetened cocoa powder
- 2 teaspoons baking powder
- 1 teaspoon salt
- 2⅔ cups sugar
- 1½ cups butter, melted
- 4 eggs
- 2 teaspoons vanilla
- 1 14-ounce package vanilla caramels, unwrapped
- 2 tablespoons milk
- 1 cup toasted hazelnuts (filberts), chopped
- 2 tablespoons hazelnut liqueur
- 2 cups dark or bittersweet chocolate pieces

WHAT YOU DO

1. Preheat oven to 350°F. Line a 13×9×2-inch baking pan with foil, extending foil over edges of pan. Generously grease foil; set pan aside. In a large bowl stir together flour, cocoa powder, baking power, and salt; set aside.

2. In an extra-large mixing bowl combine sugar and melted butter. Beat with an electric mixer on low speed until well combined. Beat in eggs and vanilla until combined. Add flour mixture, ½ cup at a time, beating well after each addition (batter will be thick). Evenly spread batter in the prepared baking pan.

3. In a large microwave-safe bowl combine caramels and milk. Microwave on 100 percent power (high) for 1½ to 2 minutes or until caramels are melted, stirring every 30 seconds. Stir in ½ cup of the hazelnuts and the liqueur. Drizzle caramel mixture over batter in pan.

4. Bake for 45 minutes. Remove from oven. Immediately sprinkle with chocolate pieces. Let stand about 2 minutes or until softened. Spread chocolate on brownies. Sprinkle with the remaining hazelnuts.

5. Cool in pan on a wire rack. (If necessary, refrigerate until chocolate sets.) Using edges of foil, lift brownies out of pan. Cut in bars. Makes 36 brownies.

To Store: Arrange brownies in a single layer in an airtight container; cover. Refrigerate up to 3 days.

White and Dark Chocolate Chunk Cookies

Shown on page 28

WHAT YOU NEED

1	cup butter, softened
¾	cup granulated sugar
¾	cup packed brown sugar
1	teaspoon baking soda
1	egg
1	teaspoon vanilla
2½	cups all-purpose flour
11	to 12 ounces white baking pieces and/or semisweet chocolate, chopped

WHAT YOU DO

1. Preheat oven to 375°F. In a large mixing bowl beat the butter with an electric mixer on medium to high speed for 30 seconds. Add granulated sugar, brown sugar, and baking soda; beat until well combined. Add egg and vanilla; beat well. Gradually beat in flour. Stir in the white baking chips and/or the chopped semisweet chocolate chunks.

2. Drop rounded teaspoons of dough 2 inches apart onto ungreased cookie sheets. Bake in preheated oven for 8 to 10 minutes or until edges are lightly browned. Transfer to wire racks and let cool.

3. If desired, dip about half of each cookie into the White Chocolate Coating or Chocolate Coating; place on waxed paper and let stand for 30 minutes or until set. Makes 4 dozen.

Double-Chocolate Chunk Cookies: Prepare recipe as above, except increase to 2 eggs. Add 2 ounces unsweetened chocolate, melted and cooled, to the egg mixture. Reduce flour to 2 cups and add ½ cup unsweetened cocoa powder. Stir

in your choice of chocolate chunks.

White Chocolate Coating: In a heavy saucepan combine 2 cups white baking pieces and 3 tablespoons shortening. Cook and stir over medium-low heat until chocolate melts. Cool slightly.

Chocolate Coating: In a heavy saucepan combine 2 cups semisweet chocolate pieces and 5 tablespoons shortening. Cook and stir over medium-low heat until chocolate melts. Cool slightly.

Fruit Dream Cookies

Shown on page 28

WHAT YOU NEED

½	cup butter, softened
½	cup shortening
1	cup granulated sugar
½	cup sugar-sweetened orange-, lemon-, or cherry-flavor drink mix
½	teaspoon baking powder
¼	teaspoon baking soda
2	eggs
1	teaspoon vanilla
2½	cups all-purpose flour
1½	cups white baking pieces
	Colored or coarse sugar

WHAT YOU DO

1. Preheat oven to 375°F. In a large mixing bowl beat butter and shortening with an electric mixer on medium to high speed for 30 seconds. Add granulated sugar, drink mix, baking powder, and baking soda. Beat until fluffy, scraping sides of bowl occasionally. Beat in eggs and vanilla until combined. Beat in as much of the flour as you can with the mixer. Stir in any remaining flour and the baking pieces. Cover and chill dough for 30 minutes or until easy to handle.

2. Shape dough in 1-inch balls. Roll in colored or coarse sugar. Place balls 2 inches apart on an ungreased cookie sheet. Bake for 9 to 11 minutes or just until edges are set (centers will still be soft). Let cool for 2 minutes on cookie sheet. Transfer to a wire rack; cool. Makes about 5 dozen.

Cardamom Snowman Cutouts

Shown on page 28

WHAT YOU NEED

1	cup butter, softened
1½	cups granulated sugar
¾	teaspoon ground cardamom
½	teaspoon baking powder
½	teaspoon salt
2	eggs
¼	cup milk
1½	teaspoons vanilla
3	cups all-purpose flour
1	recipe Royal Icing
	Black shoestring licorice
	Black and orange jelly beans, halved
	Miniature red candy-coated milk chocolate pieces
	Flaked coconut
	White ribbon

WHAT YOU DO

1. In a large mixing bowl beat butter with an electric mixer on medium to high speed for 30 seconds. Add sugar, cardamom, baking powder, and salt. Beat until combined, scraping sides of bowl occasionally. Beat in eggs, milk, and vanilla until combined. Beat in as much of the flour as you can with the mixer. Stir in any remaining flour with a wooden spoon. Divide dough in half. Cover and chill for 2 hours or until easy to handle.

2. Preheat oven to 425°F. On a lightly floured surface roll half of the dough at a time to ⅛-inch thickness. Cut dough using 2¼-, 2⅝-, and 3¹⁄₁₆-inch round cookie cutters. (By rerolling the dough, you should get about nine cutouts of each size from each dough half.) Place cutouts 1 inch apart on an ungreased cookie sheet. Using a straw, punch a hole near the edge of each 2¼-inch round. Punch two holes opposite each other in each 2⅝-inch round. Punch one hole near the edge of each 3¹⁄₁₆-inch round. Bake for 5 minutes or until edges just start to brown. Transfer to a wire rack; cool.

3. Frost cookies with Royal Icing. Decorate snowmen with licorice, jelly beans, and chocolate pieces, using the small rounds for heads and the larger rounds for bodies. Sprinkle with coconut. Allow to stand 1 hour or until set.

4. To assemble each snowman, line up one cookie of each size vertically so the holes align. Using white ribbon, tie cookie rounds together. Makes 18 snowmen.

Royal Icing: In a large mixing bowl combine one 16-ounce package powdered sugar (4½ cups), 3 tablespoons meringue powder, and ½ teaspoon cream of tartar. Add ½ cup warm water and 1 teaspoon vanilla. Beat with an electric mixer on low speed until combined; beat on high speed for 7 to 10 minutes or until mixture is very stiff. Store, covered, in refrigerator for up to 2 days. Makes about 5 cups.

Peppermint Palmiers
Shown on page 29

WHAT YOU NEED
- ½ cup butter, softened
- ½ cup granulated sugar
- ½ cup packed brown sugar
- ½ teaspoon baking powder
- ¼ teaspoon salt
- 1 egg
- 3 tablespoons white crème de menthe
- 1 tablespoon milk
- ½ teaspoon vanilla
- 2¾ cups all-purpose flour
- 1 8-ounce package cream cheese, softened
- ½ cup powdered sugar
- ¼ cup all-purpose flour
  Few drops red food coloring
- ½ cup finely crushed peppermint candies

WHAT YOU DO
1. In a large mixing bowl beat butter with an electric mixer on medium to high speed for 30 seconds. Add granulated sugar, brown sugar, baking powder, and salt. Beat until combined, scraping sides of bowl occasionally. Beat in egg, 2 tablespoons of the crème de menthe, the milk, and vanilla until combined. Beat in as much of the 2¾ cups flour as you can with the mixer. Using a wooden spoon, stir in any remaining flour. Divide dough in half. Cover and chill about 3 hours or until dough is easy to handle.

2. Meanwhile, for filling, in a medium bowl combine cream cheese, powdered sugar, the ¼ cup flour, and the remaining 1 tablespoon crème de menthe. Beat on low to medium speed until smooth. Stir in food coloring, one drop at a time, until filling is pale pink. Gently stir in crushed candies. Cover and chill up to 2 hours. (Do not chill longer than 2 hours or the candies will bleed into the filling and the filling will become too soft and sticky.)

3. On a lightly floured surface, roll half the dough at a time to a 12×8-inch rectangle. Spread with half the filling to within ½ inch of the long sides. Roll both long sides, scroll style, to meet in the center. Brush seam where spirals meet with water; lightly press together. Wrap each roll in plastic wrap or waxed paper. Freeze about 4 hours or until dough is firm enough to slice.

4. Preheat oven to 350°F. Line a cookie sheet with parchment paper; set aside. Cut rolls in ¼-inch slices. Place 2 inches apart on the prepared cookie sheet. Bake about 10 minutes or until edges are firm and bottoms are light brown. Transfer to a wire rack and let cool. Makes about 72 cookies.

Santa Cutouts
Prepare the cookie dough for the Festive Sandwich Stars on page 33. Using a 3-inch triangle-shape cookie cutter, cut out dough. Brush coat and hat areas with red Egg Paint, then bake as directed. Decorate cooled cookies with Snow Frosting, Powdered Sugar Icing, flaked coconut, and small candies. Makes about 40 Santa cookies. Shown on page 30.

Egg Paint: In a small bowl stir together 1 egg yolk and 2 drops water. Tint with red paste food coloring.

Snow Frosting: In a small bowl combine ½ cup shortening and ½ teaspoon vanilla. Beat with an electric mixer on medium to high speed for 30 seconds. Gradually add 1⅓ cups powdered sugar, beating well. Beat in 1 tablespoon milk. Gradually add 1 cup additional powdered sugar, beating well. Beat in 3 to 4 teaspoons additional milk, 1 teaspoon at a time, to make a frosting of piping consistency. After baking use a decorating bag fitted with a medium star tip to pipe frosting in areas where a textured look is desired.

Powdered Sugar Icing: In a bowl stir together 4 cups powdered sugar and 1 teaspoon vanilla. Stir in 3 to 4 tablespoons milk, 1 tablespoon at a time, to make icing of piping consistency. If desired, tint with paste food coloring. Use a decorating bag fitted with a writing tip to pipe icing.

Crisp Mini Biscotti

Shown on page 30

WHAT YOU NEED

¾	cup butter, softened
½	cup sugar
1	teaspoon baking powder
1	egg
1	teaspoon vanilla
1	cup cornmeal
1½	cups all-purpose flour
1	cup chopped pistachio nuts
2	teaspoons finely shredded orange peel
5	ounces white chocolate, coarsely chopped
1	tablespoon shortening
½	cup chopped pistachio nuts

WHAT YOU DO

1. Preheat the oven to 375°F. In a large mixing bowl beat butter with an electric mixer on medium to high speed for 30 seconds. Add sugar and baking powder; beat until combined. Beat in egg and vanilla until combined. Beat in cornmeal and as much of the flour as you can with the mixer. Stir in remaining flour, pistachios, and orange peel.
2. Shape dough in three 8×1½-inch loaves. Place loaves 4 inches apart on a large ungreased cookie sheet; flatten slightly. Bake in the preheated oven for 20 minutes or until a wooden toothpick inserted near the centers come out clean. Cool loaves on cookie sheet for 1 hour.
3. Preheat oven to 325°F. Transfer loaves to a cutting board. Cut each loaf in ½-inch-thick slices. Carefully place slices, cut sides down, on the cookie sheet. Bake for 8 minutes; gently turn over slices and bake 8 to 10 minutes more or until lightly browned. Transfer to wire racks and cool.

4. In a small saucepan melt white chocolate and shortening. Dip the top of each cookie in white chocolate mixture and sprinkle immediately with nuts. Place on waxed paper until set. Makes about 42 cookies.

Holiday Cranberry Syrup

Shown on page 31

WHAT YOU NEED

2½	cups cranberry juice
1	cup cranberries
¾	cup light-color corn syrup
¼	cup sugar

WHAT YOU DO

1. In a medium saucepan combine cranberry juice, cranberries, corn syrup, and sugar. Stir to dissolve sugar. Bring to a rolling boil over medium-high heat; reduce heat to medium. Boil gently, uncovered, for 30 to 40 minutes or until reduced to 2½ cups.
2. Pour syrup through a fine-mesh strainer or strainer lined with 100-percent-cotton cheesecloth. Discard cranberries. Cover and chill syrup at least 3 hours to cool completely or up to 1 week. Use as a base for drinks or as a topper for ice cream, cake, or pancakes. Makes 2 cups.
Cranberry-Orange Martini: Pour 1 ounce (2 tablespoons) Holiday Cranberry Syrup into a chilled martini glass. In a cocktail shaker combine ½ cup ice cubes and 1 ounce (2 tablespoons) each of orange juice and vodka. Cover and shake vigorously; slowly strain mixture into glass over the syrup. Stir mixture gently once or twice to slightly blend the layers. For a well-blended drink, add the syrup to the cocktail

shaker with the orange juice and vodka, and increase ice cubes to 1 cup. Makes 1 (4-ounce) serving.

Lemon Curd Bars

Shown on page 31

WHAT YOU NEED

1	cup butter, softened
1	cup sugar
2	cups all-purpose flour
½	teaspoon baking powder
1	10- to 12-ounce jar lemon curd
⅔	cup flaked coconut
½	cup slivered or sliced almonds or coarsely chopped pecans, toasted

WHAT YOU DO

1. Preheat oven to 375°F. Line a 13×9×2-inch baking pan with foil, extending about 1 inch of foil over the sides of pan. Grease foil; set pan aside.
2. In a large mixing bowl beat butter with an electric mixer on medium to high speed for 30 seconds. Add sugar. Beat until combined, scraping sides of bowl occasionally. Add flour and baking powder; beat until just combined and mixture resembles coarse crumbs. Reserve ⅔ cup of the crumb mixture; set aside. Press the remaining crumb mixture evenly into the bottom of the prepared pan.
3. Bake in the preheated oven for 5 to 8 minutes or until top is golden. Remove from oven. Spread lemon curd over hot crust to within ½ inch of the edges of the pan. In a medium bowl stir together reserved crumb mixture, the coconut, and almonds. Sprinkle crumb mixture on lemon curd.
4. Bake for 18 to 20 minutes more or until edges are golden and topping is brown. Cool in pan on a wire rack. Using

prevent overbrowning, cover with foil for the last 15 minutes of baking.

4. Cool in pan on a wire rack for 10 minutes. Remove from pan. Cool completely on wire rack. Wrap and store overnight before slicing. Serve with Orange Butter. Makes 1 loaf (14 slices).

Orange Butter: In a small bowl stir together ⅓ cup butter, softened; 1 tablespoon powdered sugar; and 1 teaspoon finely shredded orange peel until combined. Makes about ⅓ cup.

Little Pumpkin Cakes with Nut Brittle Shards

Shown on page 32

WHAT YOU NEED
- 1 cup all-purpose flour
- ¾ teaspoon baking powder
- ¾ teaspoon pumpkin pie spice
- ½ teaspoon salt
- ¼ teaspoon baking soda
- 2 eggs
- ¾ cup sugar
- ⅓ cup cooking oil
- ½ of a 15-ounce can pumpkin (¾ cup plus 2 tablespoons)
- Browned Butter Icing
- Caramelized Hazelnut Brittle

WHAT YOU DO

1. Preheat oven to 350°F. Grease and lightly flour or line with paper bake cups twelve 2½-inch muffin cups, four 3½-inch muffin cups, or thirty-six 1¾-inch muffin cups. Set aside. In a medium bowl stir together flour, baking powder, pumpkin pie spice, salt, and baking soda.

2. In a large bowl combine eggs, sugar, and cooking oil; beat with an electric mixer on medium speed until combined. Alternately add flour mixture and pumpkin to sugar mixture, beating just until mixture is combined.

3. Spoon batter into prepared muffin cups, filling each two-thirds full. Bake until a toothpick inserted in center comes out clean. Allow 20 to 25 minutes for 2½-inch cups, 25 to 30 minutes for 3½-inch cups, or 12 to 15 minutes for the 1¾-inch muffin cups. Cool in muffin cups on a wire rack for 5 minutes. Using a knife, loosen edges; carefully remove cakes from muffin cups. Cool completely on rack.

4. Frost cupcakes with Browned Butter Icing. Arrange shards of Caramelized Hazelnut Brittle on top of cupcakes. Makes 12 (2½-inch), 4 (3½-inch), or 36 (1¾-inch) cupcakes.

Browned Butter Icing: In a small saucepan heat 3 tablespoons butter over low heat until melted. Continue heating until butter turns a delicate brown. Remove from heat. In a large bowl combine 1½ cups powdered sugar, 1 tablespoon milk, and ½ teaspoon vanilla. Add browned butter. Beat with an electric mixer on low speed until combined. Beat on medium to high speed until it's easy to spread, adding additional milk if necessary.

Caramelized Hazelnut Brittle: Line a large baking sheet with foil; butter foil. Set aside. In a small saucepan melt 2 teaspoons butter over low heat. Stir in ⅓ cup chopped hazelnuts (filberts); keep hazelnuts warm over low heat. Place 1 cup sugar in a heavy 12-inch skillet; heat over medium-high heat until sugar begins to melt, shaking skillet occasionally to heat sugar evenly. Reduce heat to medium-low; cook until sugar melts and turns golden, stirring only as necessary after sugar begins to melt. (This should take 12 to 15 minutes.) Remove from heat; quickly stir in warm chopped hazelnuts. Immediately pour the mixture onto the prepared baking sheet, allowing syrup to flow and distributing nuts evenly. Cool completely. Break candy into shardlike pieces. Store in tightly covered container in a cool dry place up to 1 month.

Make-Ahead Directions: Prepare pumpkin cakes as directed through Step 3. Place in an airtight container; cover. Store at room temperature up to 3 days or freeze up to 1 month. Thaw cakes, if frozen. Continue as directed in Step 4.

edges of foil, lift bars out of pan. Cut in bars. Makes 32 bars.

To Store: Place bars in a single layer in an airtight container; cover. Store in the refrigerator up to 3 days.

Cranberry-Orange Loaf

Shown on page 32

WHAT YOU NEED
- 2 cups all-purpose flour
- 1 cup sugar
- 2 teaspoons baking powder
- ½ teaspoon salt
- 1 teaspoon finely shredded orange peel
- 2 eggs
- ½ cup milk
- ½ cup butter, melted
- ¾ cup coarsely chopped cranberries
- ¾ cup chopped pistachios or walnuts, toasted
- ½ cup chopped dried figs and/or dried apricots
- Orange Butter

WHAT YOU DO

1. Preheat oven to 350°F. Grease the bottom and ½ inch up sides of an 8×4×2-inch loaf pan; set aside. In a large bowl stir together flour, sugar, baking powder, and salt. Stir in orange peel. Make a well in center of flour mixture; set aside.

2. In a medium bowl beat eggs with a fork; stir in milk and melted butter. Add egg mixture all at once to flour mixture. Stir just until moistened (batter should be lumpy). Fold in cranberries, nuts, and figs and/or apricots.

3. Spoon batter into prepared pan; spread evenly. Bake for 65 to 70 minutes or until a wooden toothpick inserted near the center comes out clean. If necessary to

welcoming entrances

Your guests will be filled with the Christmas spirit the minute they see your festively decorated holiday home.

When an entry boasts two beautiful doors, dress it up with a **Double Wreath Welcome**, *left*. Hang a wreath on each door and complete the beautiful entrance with multiple ribbons and the cheery sound of jingle bells. Turn on Christmas charm with a **Beribboned Carriage Light**, *above*, all decked out with matching ribbons and bells. Instructions are on page 47.

Rest a Christmas-red gazing ball in a stone
birdbath for **Holiday Gazing**, *above*.
A wood sled serves double duty when it isn't
cruising the snow-covered hills. Just wire on
fresh greenery, pinecones, and fruit to make
a **Festive Christmas Sled**, *right*, to greet
your guests at the door.

Winter cardinals make their appearance on a purchased lantern to sing

songs of the season. A bright red bow and sprays of greenery and

berries make this **Nature's Greeting** a welcome addition to a front

entry. Instructions for all of the projects are on page 47.

Make hanging baskets sparkle all winter long by lighting them from within. These **Sparkling Starry Baskets**, *right*, hang from iron hooks near winter walkways. Old-fashioned carriage lights are decked with beads, bows, and a greeting to make a **Merry Christmas Lantern**, *right*. Beads are secured to the lantern and an oversize bow complete the look. For instructions, see page 48.

A sphere of pinecones tinted with warm tones of pink and brick red perches atop greens in a simple glazed pot. The **Pretty Pinecone Arrangement,** *above,* is easy to make and stays in style long after the holiday season is over. For instructions, see page 48.

Create a stunning **Lighted Star Welcome**, *left*, using faux greenery, acrylic snowflakes, and battery lights. Let the light of the holidays shine by wrapping tiny white bulbs around a wire form placed in a garden urn to make a **Glowing Topiary**, *below*. For instructions, see pages 48–49.

Line walkways with soft winter light by designing your own **Warm Winter Luminarias**, *right.* The designs are cut into white paper bags and the glow comes from a candle within a canning jar set inside. Add light and color around holiday windows by displaying **Sparkling Window Boxes**, *right.* The boxes are filled with greenery and tiny white lights. For instructions and patterns, see page 49.

Double Wreath Welcome
Shown on page 38

WHAT YOU NEED
2 fresh green wreaths
3-inch-wide ribbon in two colors
2 wreath hangers
2 large jingle bells
2 small jingle bells
Florist's wire

WHAT YOU DO
For each wreath: Determine the desired
length of ribbon. Cut the ribbon so it
loops around the top of the wreath twice.
Wire or sew the jingle bells to the ribbon
tails. Tie the second piece of ribbon over
the first. Trim the ends and hang the
wreaths on the wreath hangers.

Beribboned Carriage Light
Shown on page 39

WHAT YOU NEED
3 yards of 3-inch-wide ribbon in
    desired color
3 large jingle bells
Fresh greenery
24-gauge wire
Wire cutters

WHAT YOU DO
Make a large bow with long tails.
Wire the jingle bells to the center of the
bow. Set aside. Wire the greenery to the
carriage light. Wire the bow and bells
over the top of the greens.

Holiday Gazing
Shown on page 40

WHAT YOU NEED
Red gazing ball
Stone birdbath; floral tack
Fresh greenery; red berries
Large red bow

WHAT YOU DO
Secure the gazing ball in the bowl of the
birdbath using outside floral tack if
necessary. Arrange the greenery around
the ball. Add the berries and bow.

Festive Christmas Sled
Shown on page 40

WHAT YOU NEED
Fresh greenery
Pinecones
Red fruit, such as apples
Wooden sled
24-gauge wire
Red ribbon

WHAT YOU DO
Wire the greens, fruit, and pinecones
to the sled. Add a large red bow.

Nature's Greeting
Shown on page 41

WHAT YOU NEED
Purchased freestanding lantern
Fresh greenery; 24-gauge wire
Acrylic red berries; red ribbon
Glue suitable for outdoor use, such
    as E-6000
Red cardinals

WHAT YOU DO
Wire the greenery and berries at the top
of the lantern. Tie a bow on the greenery.
Glue the cardinals in place.

47

Sparkling Starry Baskets
Shown on page 42

WHAT YOU NEED
Coiled vine baskets without liners
100-bulb string or white pearl lights
Clear plastic ornaments
50-bulb string of white lights
Purchased metal star ornaments

WHAT YOU DO
Remove the liner of the coiled vine basket if necessary. Push the 100-bulb string of lights from the inside of the basket to the outside. Place the clear ornaments in the basket to fill. Add the 50-bulb string of lights. Set the metal stars on top of the lights.

Merry Christmas Lantern
Shown on page 42

WHAT YOU NEED
Outdoor lantern
Strand of Christmas beads in desired color
3-inch wide ribbon in desired color
Wire; wire cutters
Glue suitable for outdoor use, such as E6000
"Merry Christmas" hanging decoration (available at crafts and discount stores)

WHAT YOU DO
Cut the beads apart and glue to the bottom of the lantern. Tie a large bow and wire to the base of the lantern. Hang the "Merry Christmas" decoration over the top of the lantern.

Pretty Pinecone Arrangement
Shown on page 43

WHAT YOU NEED
10-inch foam ball, such as Styrofoam
Medium-size pinecones
Spray paint in pink and brick red
24-gauge wire; wire snips; ribbon
Tall square pot; fresh greenery

WHAT YOU DO
1. Lay the pinecones on a covered surface and spray with the brick red paint. Allow to dry. Spray over the brick red paint with pink paint. Allow to dry. Wire the cones and poke them into the foam ball until it is entirely covered.
2. Place greenery into the tall pot. Set the pinecone ball into the greens. Make a bow and poke into the side of the pot.

Lighted Star Welcome
Shown on page 44

WHAT YOU NEED
6-inch Styrofoam disc, 1½ inches thick
Eighteen 6- to 8-inch Lucite icicles of same pattern or 6 (foundation) of one type and 12 (support) of another
6 additional icicles
3 star ornaments
15 mini light battery light set
Small piece white poster board
3- to 4-inch decorative snowflake ornament for center
Glitter sticks (about 36)
6 snowflake ornaments about 3 inches in diameter
Faux evergreen sprigs/short 3 to 4-inch branch tips

3-inch-wide wired ribbon
Side cutter for trimming wire stems/picks
Hot-glue gun
Floral pins
2 or 3 floral picks
Scissors

WHAT YOU DO
1. Cut out a space for the battery pack to fit into the foam. Allow room to access the switch. Glue a piece of poster board over back of battery pack or the front of the piece. Cut a piece of poster board to hold pack in place from the back but to make it accessible to replace needed batteries.
2. Insert 6 foundation icicles around edge of foam, spacing to replicate a Christmas star. Place a support icicle on either side of the foundation icicle. Hot-glue in place.

3. Pin a light strand in place, spotlighting star spires and spacing lights evenly. Pin excess light cord flat. Insert glitter sticks around edge or thickness of foam disc. Insert snowflakes behind star spires. Insert decorative icicles in front of each spire at top edge of styrofoam. Arrange floral picks in center of disc and spires. Using floral pins, attach decorative snowflake ornament to center.

4. Insert and glue evergreen pieces to fill and cover styrofoam disc. Attach ribbon loop to top of disc with glue and floral pins. Cut 3 different lengths of ribbon and fold to a point at one end. Attach ribbons to bottom center of piece with glue and floral pins. Hot glue stars at end of ribbons.

Glowing Topiary
Shown on page 45

WHAT YOU NEED
Birdbath
Fresh greenery
Purchased vine ball
Battery powered lights
Green floral wire

WHAT YOU DO
Thread the strand of battery powered lights into the ball and attach with the floral wire to secure. Arrange fresh greenery in the birdbath. Set the ball and lights on top of the greens.

Sparkling Window Boxes
Shown on page 46

WHAT YOU NEED
Window boxes
Floral foam
Fresh greenery
White lights

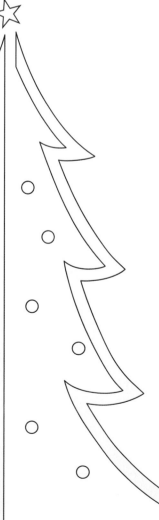

WARM WINTER
LUMINARIAS
Full-Size Pattern

WHAT YOU DO
Cut the floral foam to fit the window box. Arrange the greenery in the floral foam. Tuck lights among the greenery.

Warm Winter Luminarias
Shown on page 46

WHAT YOU NEED
Tracing paper; pencil
White paper sacks
Crafts knife
Heavy cardboard to
    fit inside the sack
Pencil
Crafts knife
Paper punch
Gold marker (optional)
Glass canning jars to fit
    inside sacks
White votive candles

WHAT YOU DO
Plan desired pattern or copy pattern, *left*. Transfer to the sack using a pencil. Put a piece of heavy cardboard in the sack. Lay the sack down on its side and using a crafts knife, paper punch, or scissors, cut out the shapes as indicated on the pattern. Draw designs around the top of the sack using the gold marker. Put the candle in the jar and put the jar inside the sack.

Never leave a burning candle unattended.

simply
handmade
holiday

Make this Christmas a special one with gifts you make yourself—and ones they will cherish forever.

Cleverly designed to be a greeting card and a holiday pin, the **Little Mitten Greeting**, *above*, is crafted from little pieces of purple wool embellished with silver seed beads. The tiny mitten is then pinned to the card for a warm greeting. Jewelry is always a favorite gift, and this lovely **Winter Beaded Necklace**, *opposite,* is no exception. The piece is made using a variety of beads in cool purples with elegant sterling beads between. Instructions are on page 62.

Tiny embellished envelopes filled with thoughtful notes make these **Message Envelope Garlands**, *above*. The notes can offer any talents to share—hours of babysitting, a manicure, or a dinner out together.

52

Taking your own bag to the store will be even more fun when the totes are so pretty and stack so beautifully. The **Stacking Eco Totes**, *below*, are made using coordinating Christmas fabrics and designed in three sizes. Instructions for all projects are on pages 62–63.

Crochet a sweet little purse for someone special. The **Classy Crocheted Clutch**, *above*, is crocheted using ribbon-style fiber and is embellished with a vintage button. Choose favorite photos and then frame them with **Folded Paper Mats**, *above*. Use lightweight scrapbook papers in fun holiday prints.

Everyone loves to have a handy kit nearby, so make your own **Pretty Mending Kit**, *left*, to give as a gift. Just fill a canning jar with sewing supplies and create a pincushion to top it off. A **Clever Beading Kit**, *left below*, holds everything needed to make a necklace and bracelet. Fill it with beads in the colors that suit the crafter. Instructions are on pages 63–64.

55

Tailor your gifts to fit each lucky recipient. Whether your gift is for one who likes to cook, watches the big screen, or favors a special food—make **Gathering Gifts** that are sure to please. Fill a bright red bowl with popcorn goodies and a movie for a **Night at Home**, *above left*. For the **Italian Lover**, *above right*, fill a green crockery baking dish with specialty pasta, favorite sauce, and cheese.

Make a **Sweet and Spicy Gift**, *below*, packed with a variety of spices for that culinary chef. Assemble a **Just for You Basket**, *below right*, complete with specialty foods and hard-to-find mixes. For more ideas for **Gathering Gifts**, see pages 64–65.

Turn simple place mats into **Pretty Place Mat Purses**, *above*, with some very clever folding techniques and a few embellishments. The sewing is minimal but the look is elegant. Purchase place mats in any color you like.

Choose small-print cottons to make **Coiled Coasters**, *above*,

that come in handy for holiday drinks. Wrap the coasters cleverly

by stacking with colorful spacers between them. Instructions are

on pages 65–66.

Simple towels turn into cute **Catch-All Baby Bibs**, *above* and *right*, that make toddler and mommy very happy. The bibs sport a Christmas motif that fits the season.

Knit dozens of these simple **Handsome Knitted Dishcloths** for everyone on your Christmas list. Choose cotton yarn to match the kitchen decor. Instructions and patterns are on pages 66–67.

14 silver flower beads
Clasp; crimp beads
Jewelry wire; jewelry tools

WHAT YOU DO

Cut wire to 20 inches. Crimp one side of clasp onto wire using crimp bead. Thread beads in this order: 3 wire, 1 silver round bead, 1 silver flower, 1 silver wire bead, 3 wire, placing a disk bead every set of 3 as shown in photograph. Crimp other side of clasp to the beaded piece using crimp bead. Secure.

Little Mitten Greeting
Shown on page 51

WHAT YOU NEED

Tracing paper; pencil
Scrap pieces of wool
2-inch piece scrap of white fur trim
2 inches cross-locked glass beads
Matching sewing thread
Purple embroidery floss
6 clear seed beads
1½ inch pin backing or safety pin
5½×8-inch piece lavender
    cardstock
3¼×5-inch piece of pink cardstock for
    inside card
2 4×1-inch pieces *each* of dark purple
    and hot pink cardstock
Scissors; decorative scissors
Gold marking pen
Crafts glue; glitter paint

WHAT YOU DO

1. Trace or copy mitten pattern onto paper and cut out. Cut two mitten patterns from wool. Using ¼-inch seam line, place right sides together and stitch around outside edges, leaving top straight edge open. Clip corners and turn right sides out.
2. Make snowflake design on front of mitten using two strands embroidery floss and straight stitches. Sew seed beads at ends of longer stitches. Sew white fur trim at top straight edge, sewing top of mitten closed. Sew glass bead string underneath white trim. Sew pin backing to back of finished mitten.

3. To make card, fold purple cardstock in half to make 4×5½-inch card. Mark cut-out shape on front and cut out shape. Using glitter paint, decorate around cut edges on card front. Trim hot pink cardstock with decorative scissors and layer under purple cardstock; glue in place. Write greeting with gold marking pen. Using crafts glue, glue pink paper underneath front cutout. Glue scrap of wool to center of pink paper. Pin mitten to wool scrap.

Winter Beaded Necklace
Shown on page 50

WHAT YOU NEED

36 wire graduated beads
28 silver round beads
3 1-inch flat disk beads

Message Envelope Garland
Shown on page 52

WHAT YOU NEED

Small envelopes; narrow ribbon
Scraps of scrapbooking paper
Small buttons; narrow ribbon
Crafts glue; paper punch

WHAT YOU DO

Cut a piece of scrapbook paper just long enough to make a strip across the envelope. Glue in place. Decorate the envelopes using small scraps of paper, ribbons, and buttons. Punch a hole at the top of each corner of each envelope. Thread the ribbon through the holes and tie together for a garland.

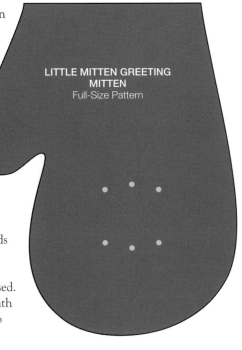

LITTLE MITTEN GREETING
MITTEN
Full-Size Pattern

LITTLE MITTEN GREETING
INSERT CUTOUT
Full-Size Pattern

Write notes about the gifts on paper and put in the envelope.

Ideas for gift notes or gifts to give:
Your gift is 3 hours of babysitting. Enjoy a night out for dinner and movie (enclose money with note). I will do your grocery shopping for 2 weeks. Your sidewalk will be shoveled by 9 a.m. for the next two snowfalls!

Stacking Eco Totes
Shown on page 53

WHAT YOU NEED
Large bag (8×11 inches):
Cotton fabric (9×25 inches) for main body of bag
2 pieces cotton fabric (4×11 inches) for side panels
Contrasting cotton fabric (4×22½ inches) for top band
2 pieces contrasting cotton fabric (3×11 inches) for handles
Medium weight fusible interfacing to back 9×25-inch piece and two 4×11-inch pieces
¾ yard medium white rickrack
Matching sewing thread

Medium Bag (7×9 inches):
Cotton fabric (8×20½ inches) for main body of bag
2 pieces cotton fabric (3½×9½ inches) for side panels
Contrasting cotton fabric (3¼×19½ inches) for top band
Medium weight fusible interfacing to back 8×20½-inch piece
1⅛ yard of ⅜-inch-wide white ribbon for band trim and handles
Matching sewing thread

Small Bag (5×6 inches):
Cotton fabric (6×14 inches) for main body of bag
2 pieces cotton fabric (3×6½ inches) for side panels
Contrasting cotton fabric (2½×14½ inches) for top band
Medium weight fusible interfacing to back 6×14-inch piece
½ yard of narrow lace trim
¾ yard of ⅛-inch cording cut into two 13½-inch lengths for handles
Matching sewing thread

WHAT YOU DO
1. Cut fabrics to sizes noted for each size of bag. Fuse interfacing to the wrong side of the fabrics to be used for the bag front and sides. Mark long sides of each bag along ½-inch seam allowances as follows: Large bag, at 11 and 14 inches; Medium bag, at 9 and 11½ inches; Small bag, at 6 and 8 inches. These markings are the points at the bottom corners of the bags.
2. Using ½-inch seam allowances and placing right sides together, sew the side pieces to the large fabric body piece, turning the corners at the markings. Clip seam allowance at corners. For handles on large bag, fold long strips together lengthwise, right sides together, and stitch. Turn right side out and press. Place handles inside of bag on front and back of bag at side seams. Baste in place with top raw edges even. For top band, place short ends right sides together and stitch side seam to make a tube. Press ¼ inch under along one long edge. Place band inside bag with right side of band facing wrong side of bag, over fabric handles (if making large bag), band seam at side of bag and top raw edges even. Stitch using ½-inch seam allowance. Turn band to outside over bag and press top seam flat. Add trim

to edge and sew down through all layers through bag body.
3. To attach handles for medium and small bags, cut ribbon or cording to lengths noted. Make small buttonholes or eyelet holes 1 inch in from sides of bags in top band area. Thread ribbon or cording lengths through holes and knot inside or outside of bag, as desired.

Folded Paper Mats
Shown on page 54

WHAT YOU NEED
Purchased picture frame with mat
Lightweight scrapbook paper
Desired photo; purchased stickers
Scissors; pencil; ruler

WHAT YOU DO
Choose the picture to be framed. It should be as tall as the opening but not as wide. Remove the glass from the picture frame. Measure the opening of the photo mat within the frame. Cut the scrapbook paper the height and width of the opening. Starting at one side, accordian pleat the paper halfway across. Lay the photo under the paper. Secure with tape. Lay the paper and photo on the glass. Frame the photo and the folded paper. Decorate with stickers.

Classy Crocheted Clutch
Shown on page 54

Skill Level: Easy
Finished Measurements:
Bag: 5" tall and 18.75" around

WHAT YOU NEED
Celebrity by Artful Yarns (JCA),
    50g/104yd balls
40% polyester/38% acrylic/22% nylon
    ribbon
1 ball in color #37
Size I/9 (5.5mm) crochet hook or size
    needed to obtain gauge.
Safety pin or stitch marker
One 1-inch-diameter button for bag

GAUGE
In sc with a double strand, 12 sts and
12 rnds = 4"/10cm.
TAKE TIME TO CHECK YOUR GAUGE.

WHAT YOU DO
Beg at the base with a double strand, ch
21, 3 sc in second ch from hook, sc in
next 18 ch, 3 sc in last ch. Working along
opposite edge, sc in 18 ch - 42 sts.
Rnd 2: (2 sc in first sc, sc in next sc,
2 sc in next sc, sc in 18 sc) twice - 46 sts.
Rnd 3: (2 sc in first sc, sc in next 3 sc,
2 sc in next sc, sc in next 18 sc) twice -
50 sts.
Rnd 4: [2 sc in first sc (sc in next 2 sc,
2 sc in next sc) twice, sc in next 18 sc]
twice - 56 sts.

BODY (place a marker on first st of rnd
and move up as you go)
Rnd 1: Sc in front lp of each st around.
Rnds 2-14: Sc in each sc around.
Rnd 15: Sc in each of the 56 sc around,
then sc in next 3 sc.
Rnd 16: Sl st in each of next 38 sc.

FLAP
Row 1: Sc in back lp of next 18 sc; turn.
Row 2: Ch 1, sk first sc, sc in next 15 sc,
sk next sc, sc in last sc - 16 sts; turn.
Row 3: Ch 1, sc in each sc across; turn.
Row 4: Ch 1, sk first sc, sc in next 13 sc,
sk next sc, sc in last sc - 14 sts; turn.
Row 5: As Row 3.
Row 6: Ch 1, sk first sc, sc in next 11 sc,
sk next sc, sc in last sc - 12 sts; turn.
Row 7: Ch 1, sk first sc, sc in next 9 sc,
sk next sc, sc in last sc - 10 sts; turn.
Row 8: Ch 1, sk first sc, sc in next 4 sc,
ch 10, sc in next 3 sc, sk next sc, sc in last
sc. Fasten off. Sew button to bag front.

Pretty Mending Kit
Shown on page 55

WHAT YOU NEED
Pencil
4-ounce canning jar with lid and band
3×3-inch piece of 1-inch-thick foam
Scissors
Thread and needle
5-inch circle of pretty fabric
2×2-inch piece of felt
Pinking shears
Thick white crafts glue
Felt scraps
Items to fill jar, such as buttons, needles,
    thread, thimble, safety pins, etc.
18 inches of ⅛-inch-wide satin ribbon
Sew-through button
½-inch gold sewing charm

WHAT YOU DO
1. Trace the widest part of the band
circle onto foam; cut out. Using thread,
gather the outside edge of the fabric
circle. Place the circle of foam onto the
top of the lid. Add the fabric circle,
pulling the gathers tightly on the
underside and allowing a ¾-inch opening.

Cut a 1½-inch felt circle with pinking
shears.
2. Glue the felt over the gathered fabric
on the underside of the lid. Smooth the
fabric over the foam, pushing the foam
away slightly at the lid edge. Add the band.
3. Fill the jar with desired sewing
notions. Put on the top. Thread a button
and tie around the jar. Tie the ribbon
ends into a bow.

Clever Beading Kit
Shown on page 55

WHAT YOU NEED
Small tin
Alphabet stickers
Holiday sticker
Crafts glue
Narrow ribbon; scissors
Beading items to fill tin

WHAT YOU DO
Glue the ribbon about 1 inch from the
bottom of the tin top. Spell out BEAD
KIT with alphabet stickers. Place the
holiday sticker on the tin. Fill the tin
with beads, jewelry wire, and crimp beads.

Gathering Gifts
Shown on pages 56–57

WHAT YOU DO
For each Gathering Gift, first choose a
container to put the items into. The
Italian Lover gift is in a green crockery

bowl suitable for a baked casserole. The Sweet and Spicy gift is in a purchased printed round box. The Just for You gift is in a basket with a handle. The Night at Home gift is in a round popcorn bowl. Choose items that fit the theme and then cushion the items with purchased shred, garland, tissue, towels, or other decorative items. Add a bow and gift tag.

Pretty Place Mat Purses
Shown on page 58

WHAT YOU NEED FOR EACH PURSE
Two 13×9-inch rectangular place mats (stiff ones work best)
Matching sewing thread
Chain belt or necklace (one large belt can make two 25-inch handles)
Clear nylon thread; straight pins

For red purse:
1 yard of ⅜-inch-wide red velvet ribbon

For gold purse:
One magnetic purse clasp
Decorative button or pin; fabric glue

WHAT YOU DO
For Red Purse:
1. Lay first place mat flat on work surface, with wrong side up, placing short edge in front of you. Fold bottom edge up 6½ inches. See Photo A. Machine stitch through all thicknesses around sides and bottom edge, over existing stitching of place mat. (A heavy denim needle works well to sew over thick, multiple layers.)
2. Lay second place mat on work surface with wrong side up, placing short edge in front of you. Fold the bottom short edge up 6¾ inches. See Photo B.
3. Machine-stitch down side edges only, through all thicknesses. Place the second

place mat on top of the first place mat with the second place mat's folded edge just meeting the folded and sewn section of the first place mat. See Photo C.
4. Fold the bottom of the first place mat up over the folded and sewn section of the second place mat. Pin along the side edges and sew through all thicknesses. Fold top flap down over front of purse.

Handle: If using a belt, take links apart to make desired length for handle (25 inches). Thread velvet ribbon in and out of links. Fold under ribbon ends and hand sew with a few stitches using matching thread. Position handle at top sides of purse, just underneath fold of front flap.

Tack chain to sides by sewing by hand using nylon thread. See Photo D.

For Gold Purse:
1. Lay first place mat flat on work surface, with wrong side up, placing short edge in front of you. Fold bottom edge up 2 inches. See Photo E, *page 66.*
2. Attach bottom magnetic snap at center of this first place mat, underneath fold and 1 inch from the fold line. Stitch across bottom section to enclose snap, stitching ¼ inch from loose edge.
2. Place right side of second place mat over wrong side of first place mat, placing bottom edge of second place mat ¼ inch up from the bottom folded up edge of the

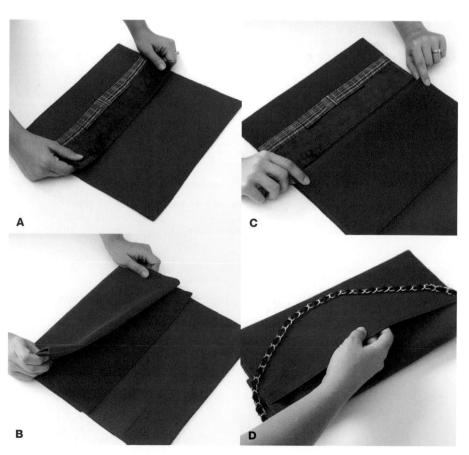

A

B

C

D

first place mat. Machine-stitch down both sides, through all thicknesses. Fold bottom edge up 8½ inches and start stitching sides 2¼ inches from top fold line. See Photo F.

3. Attach top magnetic snap at center of top flap, placing it 1 inch from the edge. Pin decorative pin or glue on large decorative button to cover back side of top snap.

Handle: If using a belt, take links apart to make desired length for handle (25 inches). Position handle at top sides of purse, just beneath fold of front flap. Tack chain to sides by sewing by hand using nylon thread. See Photo G.

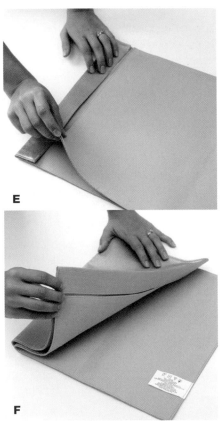

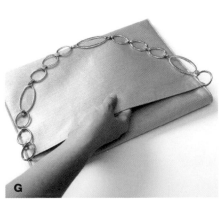

Coiled Coasters
Shown on page 59

WHAT YOU NEED
Scraps of cotton fabrics
10 feet of 3⁄16-inch-wide clothesline
Glue stick
Sewing thread of matching or contrasting color; straight pins

WHAT YOU DO
1. Cut fabric into ½- to ¾-inch strips. Cut clothesline into 54-inch pieces for each coaster. Using the glue stick, rub glue over the back of fabric for about an inch to secure. Enclose cut end of clothesline by wrapping fabric over end and around. See Photo A.
2. Continue to wrap fabric over and around length of clothesline. See Photo B. Rub glue stick over back of fabric every 4 or 5 inches and at end of length.
3. To start next length of fabric, rub glue stick over back side of the end of the new strip and overlap with last strip wrapped over clothesline. Continue gluing and wrapping to cover entire length of line. Finish out end by gluing back of last

length of fabric and covering over and around end of clothesline.
4. Coil wrapped clothesline in a tight circle and pin in place. Machine-sew end together with zigzag stitch. Continue coiling length of covered cord around and around, zigzag stitching over edge of coil to the left and coil to the right to stitch together. Secure stitching at the end as the end is tapered in to finish.

Catch-All Baby Bibs
Shown on page 60

WHAT YOU NEED FOR ONE BIB
1 kitchen dish towel (approximately 15×24 inches)
1 yard double-fold bias tape
Scraps cotton fabrics for appliqué
Fusible webbing
Scraps ribbon and rickrack trims
½ yard medium pink rickrack (for teal gingerbread bib)
Tracing paper and black embroidery floss (for blue reindeer bib)
Matching sewing threads; straight pins

WHAT YOU DO
1. With right side of dish towel facing up and lying lengthwise, fold bottom edge up (for pockets) and top edge back (approximately 5 inches to make neck and armholes), folding so length is approximately 15 inches. Pin folds in place.
2. Mark placement for appliqué shapes. Trace or copy appliqué patterns, *opposite*. Trace onto fusible webbing paper and fuse to the back of appliqué fabrics. Cut out shapes and fuse to location marked on bibs. Machine zigzag stitch around

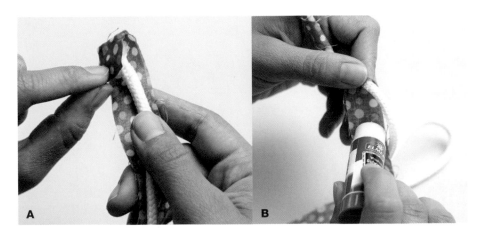

appliqué shapes (making sure to unfold teal bib at bottom so stitching is only through the single layer of backing towel). Add ribbon and rickrack trims. For reindeer bib, mark antler lines by placing tracing paper onto bib and tracing over pattern lines. Using 3 strands of black embroidery floss, stitch over lines for antlers, using stem outline stitch.

3. To make bottom pockets, securely stitch at side edges through both towel layers (a 3-step machine zigzag stitch is very strong). To make two pocket divisions, stitch again at the center of the bottom through both layers. To make three pocket divisions, mark bottom folded section in thirds and stitch twice through both layers to secure.

To make neck and armhole openings, turn bib to back side and cut down center of back flap from bottom hem of towel to top horizontal fold. Stop cut at fold and continue cutting perpendicular along top folded edge, 3½ inches to either side of center cut. This provides the neck opening and back section of bib.

4. Stitch double-fold bias tape to short ends of cut (first center cut made to top fold line), folding in tape ends at finished towel edges. To apply tape to neck opening, mark a 9-inch length (for one end to tie) and then begin pinning tape to towel neck edge, over tape end previously stitched on back flap. Pin in a continuous line from cut edge of back flap, around curve where cut stops, around front of bib, around curve of other cut, and to opposite side of back flap. Fold in cut ends of tape and stitch in one continuous line of stitching.

Securely stitch back flap to side of bib at hemmed corners to make armhole openings.

Handsome Knitted Dishcloths
Shown on page 61

Skill Level: Beginner

WHAT YOU NEED
Lily Sugar 'n' Cream, worsted weight, 100% cotton yarn; One ball each of Yellow (00010), Rose Pink (00046), and Teal (01133)

Size 8 (5mm) knitting needles or size needed to obtain gauge

GAUGE
In Garter Stitch (knit every row),
16 stitches = 4"/10 cm.
TAKE TIME TO CHECK YOUR GAUGE

WHAT YOU DO
Cast on 45 stitches. Knit every row until piece measures approximately 9½ inches from beginning. Bind off. Weave in loose ends on one side of fabric. Make one dishcloth in each color.

CATCH-ALL BABY BIBS
Full-Size Patterns

Make this Christmas oh-so-pretty with
big ideas that come in small packages.

have yourself
a pretty little
christmas

Be eco-friendly by decorating a small potted Christmas tree this year.

After the holidays, plant the tree outdoors and watch it grow. Wrap up

some **Mini Gifted Trims**, *above*, to hang on the little tree. Use lightweight

wrapping paper and narrow ribbon on small boxes or little cubes of plastic

foam. Then add **Simple Circle Ornaments**, *opposite*, made from

colorful scrapbook papers. Have fun decorating each one differently

with glitter and other trims. Instructions are on page 78.

Let your crafting green thumb create cottage charm with a little **Rosy Flower Garland**, *above*. Grown on a vine of yarn, the blooms and leaves are made of felt. A small-scale **Stocking Package Trim**, *opposite*, tags along as a charming decoration. The detail on the little stocking is made using beads and decorative stitches. This pint-size gift tag will later serve as a sweet tree decoration. Tiny beads are assembled in candylike fashion on headpins to make sweet **Candy Beaded Earrings**, *left*. Use the same technique to create a matching necklace fob. Instructions are on pages 78–81.

For plants to give as gifts or house plants for your holiday decor, wrap **Paper Planters,** *right,* in pretty containers of paper and ribbon. Cover the box first then slide a little potted plant into the container.

Individual crystal-glass salt shakers hold tiny herbs and serve as a backdrop for monogrammed place cards. The **Shaker Place Cards**, *left,* can then be given to guests as a table favor. An inexpensive flour-sack towel becomes worthy of holiday display with a few stitches. The **Little Tree Towel**, *bottom left,* makes a perfect addition to a gift basket of personal items or for holiday decorating anywhere. Instructions are on pages 80–81.

Create a **Tiny Winter Forest**, *opposite,* using winter-green printed scrapbook papers. The trees are shaped with curled edges and combine to make a wonderful holiday grouping. Roll up some scraps of ribbon to make **Elegant Ribbon Roses**, *above,* to use as package toppers. Or tuck them into fresh evergreens to add color and texture. Instructions are on pages 81–82.

75

Choose a favorite tiny quilt pattern and stitch **Mini Quilted Greeting Cards,** *opposite* and *above,* that are sure to become treasured gifts. The little quilts are matted inside the card and can be framed to showcase them later. Make your own pattern or choose designs shown on pages 84–85. Instructions and patterns are on pages 83–85.

2. Overlap and wrap outside edges at the slit and glue paper with crafts glue. Glue cone shape onto larger circle. Experiment by using different cut edges, layering papers together, placing cones on each side of a larger circle, and using different color combinations.

3. Embellish with fine glitter by using white glue to make dots, snowflake designs, and lines, as desired. Poke small hole in outside edge of ornaments using point of an awl tool. Thread cording through holes and tie ends together.

Mini Gifted Trims
Shown on pages 68–69

WHAT YOU NEED
Small boxes or cubes of plastic foam
Lightweight wrapping paper
Transparent tape
Narrow ribbon; crafts glue

WHAT YOU DO
Wrap the boxes with the wrapping paper. Tie a bow around the wrapped gifts. Make a loop from the ribbon and glue to the top of each wrapped gift for a hanger.

Simple Circle Ornaments
Shown on pages 68–69

WHAT YOU NEED
Tracing paper; pencil
Heavyweight decorative papers
Crafts glue
Pinking shears and straight-edge scissors
White glue
Extra-fine glitter
Awl
Fine metallic cording

WHAT YOU DO
1. Trace or copy circle patterns, *below*, onto paper and cut out. Trace circles onto decorative papers. Cut out circles using pinking shears or scissors. To make a three-dimensional cone shape, cut a slit into the circle, cutting from outside edge to the center of the circle.

Stocking Package Trim
Shown on page 70

WHAT YOU NEED
Tracing paper; pencil; scissors
Water-soluble marking pen
8×10-inch piece of white wool felt
Decorative-edge scissors
Scrap of wool felt in a contrasting color
DMC embroidery floss (see Color Key on Pattern, *opposite*)
Embroidery hoop
Needles: embroidery and beading
Decorative beads: orange flower and red flat circle
Assorted seed beads: red, pink, and orange
Ribbons: ¼-inch-wide check and ¾-inch-wide stripe
Fabric glue

WHAT YOU DO
1. Trace or copy the pattern, *opposite*, onto tracing paper; cut out. Using the water-soluble marking pen, trace the

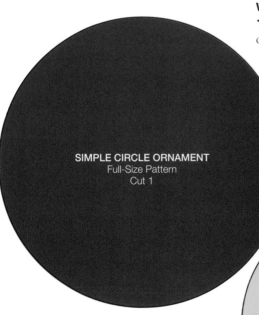

SIMPLE CIRCLE ORNAMENT
Full-Size Pattern
Cut 1

SIMPLE CIRCLE ORNAMENT
Full-Size Pattern
Cut 1 with slit
Cut 1 without slit

Slit

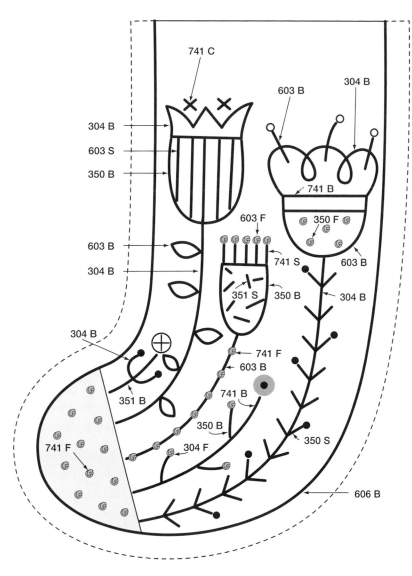

STOCKING PACKAGE TRIM

BEAD KEY
○ Orange Seed Bead
⊕ Orange Flower Bead
● Pink Seed Bead
◉ Red Flat Circle Bead

STITCH KEY
B Backstitch
C Cross Stitch
F French Knot
S Straight

COLOR KEY
304 – Red
350 – Bright Coral
351 – Coral
603 – Pink
606 – Bright Orange
741 – Yellow-Orange

Candy Beaded Earrings
Shown on page 70

WHAT YOU NEED
2 silver-lined red size 8-0 beads
2 4×8mm clear or green disk beads
1 red bead, either 8mm round or
　6×9mm cathedral shape
1 2-inch headpin
1 4-6mm O-ring
Earring findings or lobster-claw clasp

WHAT YOU DO
1. Assemble the beads on the headpin as follows: silver-lined red bead; disk bead; red round or cathedral bead; disk bead; silver-lined red bead.
2. Using the round-nose pliers, make a wrapped loop above the last bead. Cut any excess wire close to the wrap.
3. Attach to the O-ring and then to either the earring finding or the lobster-claw clasp.

pattern outline for a stocking front and a stocking back onto the white felt, leaving 1 inch between shapes. Do not cut out. Trace and cut out a stocking toe from the contrasting color of felt.
2. Tape the pattern to a sunny window or light box; place the traced stocking front on top. Transfer the embroidery design with the marking pen.
3. Baste the felt toe to the stocking front. *Note:* For embroidery-stitch instructions, refer to the diagrams on page 159.
4. Use three strands of floss for all stitching. Referring to the pattern stitch the design using the colors and stitches indicated, except do not backstitch the stocking outline.
5. To attach the flower bead, thread the beading needle with floss; bring it up through the felt at the top of the stem. Add the bead and a small red seed bead.

Bring the needle back down through the flower bead to the wrong side of the felt, and secure the thread. Attach the flat circle bead with a pink seed bead in the same way at the top of the other stem. When all stitching and beading is finished, cut out the stocking front and the stocking back, cutting at least ½ inch from the traced lines.
6. Assemble the ornament by placing the stocking front and back together with wrong sides together. Backstitch along the outline, leaving the top edge open. Use decorative-edge scissors to trim the edge of the stocking.
7. Form a hanging loop with the ¼-inch check ribbon, gluing the ends on the outside of the stocking. Glue the ¾-inch stripe ribbon around the top of the stocking for a cuff, covering the ends of the narrower ribbon. Let the glue dry.

Rosy Flower Garland

Shown on page 71

WHAT YOU NEED

Felted 100-percent-wool sweaters;
green, light green, chartreuse, red,
pink, orange, and white (see the
felting instructions on page 158.)
Size G crochet hook
Reynolds Blizzard yarn: Light Green (680)
Tracing paper; pencil
Felt: green, light green, red, pink,
orange, and white
Rigid foam insulation scrap
Felting tool
Pen-style needle-felting tool
Light green wool roving
Darning needle
Embroidery floss in colors
to match felt

WHAT YOU DO

1. Felt the sweaters by placing the
100-percent-wool sweaters in the
washing machine. (See page 158 for
Tips for Felting Wool.) Set aside.
2. To crochet the vine, use the light
green yarn and crochet hook, working
chain stitches to the desired length.

3. To make the leaves, trace or copy the
pattern, *below*, onto tracing paper; cut
out. Cut assorted leaves from the felted
green sweaters and green felt. Stack a
sweater leaf with a felt leaf and place
them on the foam insulation. Repeatedly
press the felting tool down over the
leaves. The barbed needles will integrate
the fibers of the two leaves.
4. Lay a line of wool roving down the
center of the leaf; using the pen-style
needle-felting tool, needle-felt it in place.
Alternate color combinations and make
some leaves that are made with only two
green sweater colors.
5. Using 6 strands of light green
embroidery floss and the darning needle,
stitch a pair of leaves to the yarn chain.
Continue adding leaves every 5 inches
along chain.
6. To cut the rose strips, cut a ¾-inch-
wide outer, middle, and inner strip of felt
for each rose. Cut to lengths as follows:
5¼-inch piece for the outer, 3½-inch
piece for the middle, and 2¾-inch piece
for the inner. Stack the strips from the

longest to shortest with the outer (longest)
strip on the bottom. Align one short end
of one middle and one inner strip; place
the aligned ends ½ inch from one short
end of the outer strip. This ½-inch area
will be referred to as the flap.
7. To create the roses, start rolling from
the short end opposite the flap. Roll the
thicknesses to form the rose, trapping the
ends of the inner and middle strips within
the outer strip. Using 6 strands of the
matching floss and the darning needle,
stitch through the flap and across the
rose. Return the needle back to and
through the flap to complete the stitch
and to hold all layers in place. Thread the
needle through the yarn chain directly
below the first set of leaves. Do not tie off
the thread or remove the needle. Roll the
next rose, then use the threaded darning
needle to stitch through the new rose as
directed for the first rose and attach it to
the garland; tie off the thread. Add
two roses to each leaf set.

Paper Planter

Shown on page 72

WHAT YOU NEED

Christmas cards, wrapping paper,
or other paper to cover box
Small cardboard box
Crafts glue; transparent tape
1-inch-wide grosgrain ribbon

WHAT YOU DO

If using Christmas cards, cut to fit the
sides of the box and glue in place. If using
wrapping paper, glue or wrap and tape the
paper in place. Tie a bow around the box.
Place the small plant or tree in the box.

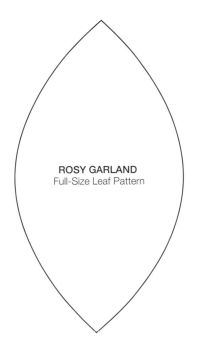

ROSY GARLAND
Full-Size Leaf Pattern

Shaker Place Cards
Shown on page 73

WHAT YOU NEED
Small glass salt shaker
Green food coloring
Fresh herbs
Green cardstock
Scrap of cream-color cardstock
Crafts glue
Purchased rhinestone initial sticker
   (available at crafts stores)

WHAT YOU DO
1. Be sure the shaker is clean and dry.
Fill with water and add a tiny drop of
green food coloring. Place a sprig of
parsley, sage, or other herb in the water.
2. To make the place card, fold the green
cardstock in half. Glue the cream-color
cardstock to the front of the green paper.
Press or adhere the initial sticker to the
place card.

Little Tree Towel
Shown on page 73

WHAT YOU NEED
Tracing paper
Water-soluble marking pen
Pink flour-sack towel
Embroidery hoop
Embroidery needle
DMC embroidery floss: 1 skein
   each of white, brown (3863),
   dark green (367), light green
   (369), and burgundy (815)
White four-hole buttons: one ¾-inch
   and one 1-inch

WHAT YOU DO
1. Copy or trace pattern, *below*, on
tracing paper. Tape the pattern to a sunny
window or light box. Tape the towel
over the pattern, centering the design
2¼ inches from the bottom (front edge
of the towel). Using the marking pen,
trace the pattern onto the towel.
Note: For embroidery-stitch instructions,
refer to the diagrams on page 159. Use
all 6 strands of floss for all embroidery.
2. Place the towel in the embroidery
hoop. Stitch white running stitches for
the snow mounds; brown satin stitches
for the tree trunk; and long, thin dark
green cross-stitches across the width of
the tree. Referring to the photo on page
73 and to the pattern, add 5 or 6 light
green straight stitches diagonally over the
cross-stitches on the tree (the straight
stitches get shorter as you work from the
bottom to the top of the tree).

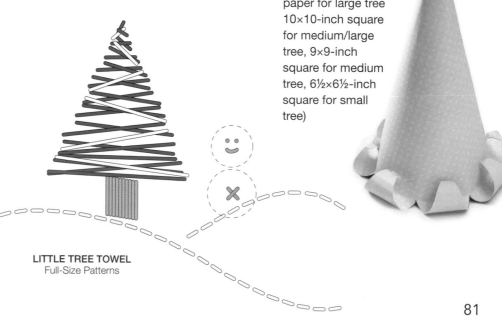

LITTLE TREE TOWEL
Full-Size Patterns

Note: When working the tree, do not
carry your embroidery threads across the
back of your work.
3. For the snowman, attach buttons as
indicated by broken-line circles on the
pattern using embroidery stitches to
secure. On the 1-inch body button, stitch
a burgundy cross-stitch through the holes.
On the ¾-inch head button, use a
burgundy straight stitch for the mouth
and two brown French knots for eyes.
Carefully press the finished piece.

Tiny Winter Forest
Shown on page 74

WHAT YOU NEED
Tracing paper; pencil
Assorted green decorative
   papers for tree tops
   (one 12×12-inch square
   paper for large tree
   10×10-inch square
   for medium/large
   tree, 9×9-inch
   square for medium
   tree, 6½×6½-inch
   square for small
   tree)

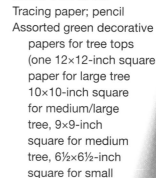

Double-sided tape
Hot-glue gun, glue sticks

WHAT YOU DO

Enlarge and trace or copy desired patterns, *below*, onto tracing paper and cut out. Trace around patterns onto green paper and cut out shapes for trees. Wrap straight ends of tree around to make a cone shape. Overlap long straight edges slightly and adhere with double-sided tape. Curl points at bottom of tree shape around a pencil to flip up ends. Tack curled points to sides of cone tree with a dot of hot glue. Hold in place until dried.

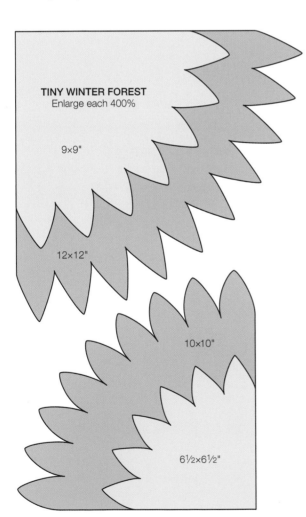

TINY WINTER FOREST
Enlarge each 400%

9×9"

12×12"

10×10"

6½×6½"

Elegant Ribbon Roses
Shown on page 75

WHAT YOU NEED

6-inch length of ribbon (wire-edge or nonwire-edge) in desired color
12-inch length of wire-edge ribbon in desired color
Small piece of green non-wired ribbon
Fine wire
Crafts glue; scissors; fine wire

WHAT YOU DO

Note: Roses can be made using two colors or a single color of ribbon.

1. Roll the shorter piece of ribbon from the short end until tightly rolled for the inside of the rose. See Diagram 1.

2. Lay out the longer piece of ribbon and gather one side of the ribbon by pulling the wire in the ribbon. Let the wire extend on both ends of the ribbon. See Diagram 2.

3. Lay the rolled inside of the rose at one end of the longer ribbon and begin rolling up the rose. Glue at the bottom to secure. See Diagram 3.

4. Cut a 4-inch length of green ribbon. Angle the ends. Wrap the middle with a small piece of wire. Glue the wrapped rose to the ribbon. See Diagram 4. Allow to dry.

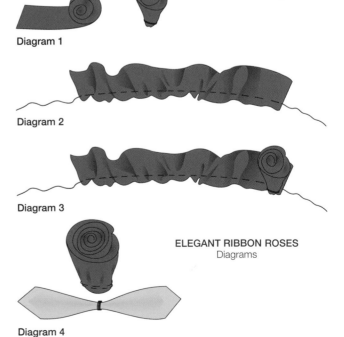

Diagram 1

Diagram 2

Diagram 3

Diagram 4

ELEGANT RIBBON ROSES
Diagrams

Mini Quilted Greeting Cards

Shown on pages 76–77

WHAT YOU NEED

Purchased flap greeting cards and
    envelopes or 12×12-inch square of
    cardstock to make card
Tracing paper or copier; pencil
Fabric scraps in desired colors
Scissors; sewing thread to match
    fabrics
Sewing machine; iron; mat paper
Transparent tape; double-stick tape
Gold marking pen; sticker (optional)

WHAT YOU DO

1. Purchase card envelope or make one
from cardstock. To make the envelope,
enlarge and trace or copy pattern, *below.*
Cut out and fold on dotted lines. Set aside.
2. Choose design and trace or copy
patterns, pages 83–85. Sew specific quilt

MINI QUILTED GREETING CARDS
Crazy House Block Pattern

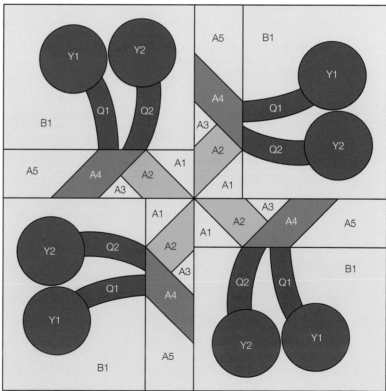

MINI QUILTED GREETING CARDS
Cherry Twirl Block Pattern

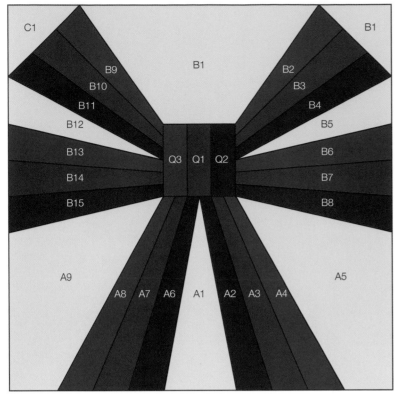

MINI QUILTED GREETING CARDS
Double Bow Block Pattern

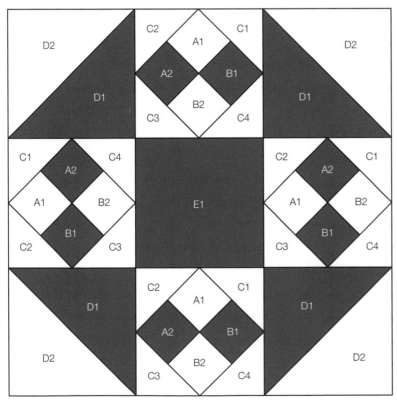

MINI QUILTED GREETING CARDS
Triangle Check Block Pattern

block as indicated. Press. Cut mat paper to fit or have professionally cut.

3. Place mini quilt into mat and adhere to back with tape. Use double-stick tape to adhere to center of card.

4. Write message on card. Close card and, if desired, add sticker to hold.

Crazy House (Squares in the middle)

Join A1 and A2 to make 8 A sections. Join into 4 A-A units. Make 4 B sections. Join sections into 3 rows (A-B-A, B-C-B, A-B-A). Join the 3 rows.

Cherry Twirl

Make 4 A sections by joining the A pieces in numerical order. Appliqué the Q1 and Q2 pieces to the four B1 pieces. Join the 4 A sections to the 4 B sections. Join the 4 A-B units. Make 8 cherries by cutting 1-inch fabric circles. Cut a cardboard circle the size of a penny and gather each fabric circle around the cardboard. Remove the cardboard and insert a small amount of batting. Appliqué the cherries to the block. Add a tiny stitch in each cherry to dimple.

Double Bow

Make the A section by joining the A pieces in numerical order. Make the B section. Join the C1 pieces to the B section. Join the A section to the B-C unit. Join the Q pieces. Appliqué the Q section to the center of the A-B-C unit.

Triangle Check

Make 4 A sections and 4 B sections. Join into 4 A-B units. Join C pieces to each side of each unit to make 4 A-B-C units. Make 4 D sections. Join a D section to each side of an A-B-C unit twice for 2 rows of the block. Join 2 A-B-C units to the E1 piece to make the center row. Join the 3 rows to complete the block.

Tree Square

Make 4 A sections by joining the A pieces in numerical order. Make 4 B sections. Join A and B sections to make 4 A-B units. Join the 4 units to make the center square. Make 4 C sections and 4 D sections. Join C sections to opposite ends of 2 D sections. Join the other 2 D sections to opposite sides of the A-B square. Join the 3 units to complete the block.

Posy Basket

Make the A section by joining the A pieces in numerical order. Appliqué the Q1 piece to the B1 piece, then join the A and B sections. Appliqué the flowers (Q2, Q3, and Q4) in place. Sew a small button to the center of each flower.

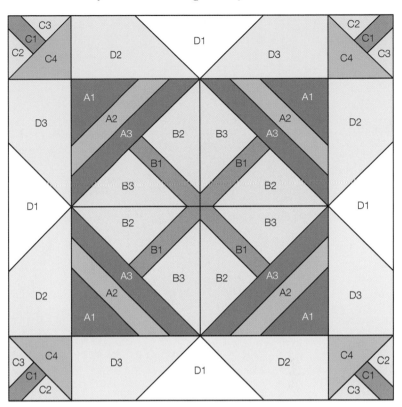

MINI QUILTED GREETING CARDS
Tree Square Block Pattern

MINI QUILTED GREETING CARDS
Posy Basket Block Pattern

Let the winter's wonderland of snow inspire you to add shimmer and frosty sparkle to your holiday decorating.

let it snow

Bring the beauty of winter, not the cold, inside with **Frosty Pearl Icicles**, *opposite* and *above,* to adorn your holiday tree. The sparkling icicles are topped with a dusting of white seed beads. Instructions are on page 96.

Set a warm hot-chocolate treat on **Warm Snowman Coasters**, *above*, made from colorful felt. Simple embroidery stitches outline the details. Instructions are on page 96.

Stack tiny round beads to make **Snowman Beaded Earrings and Zipper Pull,** *left* and *above.* Use crackle beads to make the little round balls seem even more winterlike. Instructions are on pages 96–97.

You'll hum "White Christmas" as you fold and trim **Pretty Paper Snowflakes**, *above* and *opposite,* made from printed scrapbook papers. Each snowflake uses the same basic techniques, yet no two are alike! Use them to adorn your holiday tree or group them on a silver tray. Instructions are on pages 97–98.

Let a happy **Snowman Card Holder**, *opposite,* organize your cards
or ornaments. Made from felt, this clever holder becomes a favorite
piece to set out anywhere. Sure to stack up just right, this **Paper
Box Frosty,** *above,* is not only fun to look at but also holds holiday
treasures. Instructions and patterns are on pages 98–99.

An assortment of winter-blue canning jars, acrylic snowflakes, and freshly fallen snow create a **Warm Winter Welcome**, *opposite*. Little button snowmen make a **Let it Snow Greeting**, *below*. Pure and white sparkling glitter finishes the snowy scene. Instructions are on page 99.

Frosty Pearl Icicles

Shown on page 87

WHAT YOU NEED

Assorted pearls as per chart, *below*
24-gauge beading wire
Wire cutters; rosary pliers
Small bowls or paper plates
Assorted white seed beads sizes 11-14
Jewelry/metal glue, such as Aleene's
Decorative metallic S hangers

WHAT YOU DO

1. String pearls according to the chart for the size of icicle desired onto a 10-inch piece of wire with a small short circular coil at one end (made with rosary pliers).
2. After stringing succession of beads, make another coil with rosary pliers at the top of the icicle.
3. Using small bowls, pour seed beads into dish. Drizzle glue around the top of the icicle as if dripping or melting. Roll the icicle in the small beads until glue picks up enough beads to cover glue. Set aside to dry.
4. When dry, attach decorative hangers.

	XL	L	M	S	XS
20mm	1	1			
18mm	1	1			
16mm	1	1	1	1	1
12mm	1	1	1	2	1
10mm	4	3	3	2	1
8mm	3	3	3	3	2
6mm	3	3	5	3	2
5mm	4	3	3	4	2
3.5mm	5	3	5	4	2

Warm Snowman Coasters

Shown on page 88

WHAT YOU NEED

Wool felt (white, black, rust, blue, red)
Tracing paper
Pencil; scissors
Sewing thread (black, rust, blue)
Embroidery floss (black, white)

WHAT YOU DO

1. Wash and dry the felt to felt the fabric. (See page 158 for felting tips.) Felting the fabric shrinks it and gives it a soft crinkled texture. Set the fabric aside.

2. Trace or copy the full-size patterns, *below*, onto tracing paper. For each coaster, cut 2 each of large circle from white felt. Cut remaining eyes, nose, and scarf pieces. Straight-stitch close to outside edges to attach eyes, nose, and scarf pieces onto one white felt circle.
3. Using 3 strands of black embroidery floss, stitch mouth using running stitch. Place white circle back piece beneath top face piece. With 3 strands of white embroidery floss, use the blanket stitch (see diagram on page 159) to hold the two pieces together, flipping up bottom edge of scarf to stitch bottom edges of circles together.
4. Cut 5 or 6 slits in on the edge of the scarf to fringe the scarf end.

Snowman Beaded Earrings and Zipper Pull

Shown on page 89

WHAT YOU NEED

1 12mm clear round crackle bead
1 8mm clear round crackle bead
1 6mm clear round crackle bead
1 4mm black disk (or any flat 4mm black bead)
1 size 6-0 black bead
1 2-inch headpin

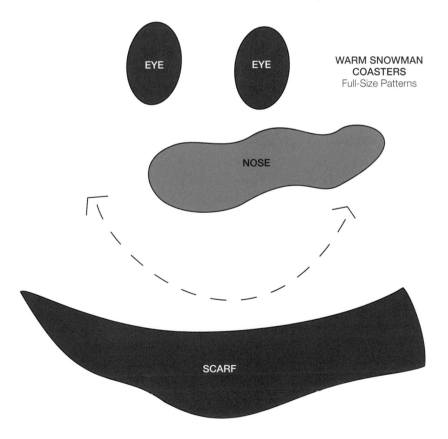

WARM SNOWMAN COASTERS
Full-Size Patterns

EYE   EYE

NOSE

SCARF

1 4-6mm O-ring
Earring findings or lobster-claw clasp
Round-nose pliers
Wire cutters

WHAT YOU DO

1. Assemble beads onto headpin in the order listed.
2. Using round-nose pliers, make a wrapped loop above the last bead. Cut any excess wire close to the wrap.
3. Attach to O-ring and then to each earring finding or lobster-claw clasp.

Pretty Paper Snowflakes
Shown on pages 90–91

WHAT YOU NEED

Assorted decorative papers or
    scrapbook papers
Double-sided tape; white glue
Decorative-edge scissors or
    pinking shears
Silver glitter or glitter glue
Needle and thread; crafts glue
Assorted sequins, beads, jewels
Awl; fine silver cording

WHAT YOU DO

1. Cut paper into strips to make three different sizes of snowflake ornaments:
Small: 1½×14¼ inches (make ¾-inch folds for 10 points total)
Medium: 2×14½ inches (make 1-inch folds for 7 points total)
Large: 2½×25 inches long (make 1¼-inch folds for 9 points total)

A

B

C

HEAD

**WARM SNOWMAN
COASTERS**
Full-Size Pattern

2. Cut paper into desired width of strips, using straight or decorative edge scissors. Fold paper accordion-fold manner, making folds to size indicated to achieve size and number of points desired. See Photo A on page 97. Wrap strip around to form a loop, checking for the number of complete points and making sure to have a little overlap to connect paper ends. While still in a long strip, fold together one pleat and angle cut each fold to make a point or rounded arc for the ends of the snowflakes. Make additional notches or cuts in folds to get open design desired. Add glitter to decorate as desired, using white glue and fine glitter or glitter glue. Let dry.

3. Tape or glue ends of accordion-pleated strip together to form a loop. Bring flat ends together in center and flatten strip to fan out pointed ends at the outside. See Photo B on page 97.

4. Working from back side, stitch folds together with needle and double thread, drawing thread together tightly to cinch up the center back. Turn shape over to the front and sew folds together again. See Photo C on page 97.

5. Glue sequin or other trim onto center of snowflake to cover where points meet and let dry. Make a small hole in the end of one point using an awl. Thread length of fine cording through hole and tie ends together to hang.

Snowman Card Holder

Shown on page 92

WHAT YOU NEED

Tracing paper; pencil
13×22-inch piece of one-sided
    fusible Peltex stabilizer
13×22-inch piece of white
    fleece or felt
Scrap of orange fleece or felt
    for carrot nose
Scrap of purple fleece or felt
    for earmuffs
Small amount Polyfil stuffing
2 1×16-inch strips of stiffened
    black glitter felt for handle
2 1-inch black shank buttons
    for eyes
5 ½-inch black shank
    buttons for mouth

White sewing thread
Black sewing thread
Needle and matching sewing threads
    for earmuffs and nose
Fabric glue
4 paper fasteners (brads)
Awl

WHAT YOU DO

1. Trace or copy and enlarge all patterns onto paper and cut out. Fuse Peltex to back of white fleece. Trace basket side and bottom patterns onto back of Peltex and cut out. Using white sewing thread, zigzag stitch over top curvy edge of basket. Curve basket around and join

SNOWMAN CARD HOLDER NOSE
Full-Size Pattern
Cut 2

SNOWMAN CARD HOLDER EARMUFF
Full-Size Pattern
Cut 4

SNOWMAN CARD HOLDER BASKET
Full-Size Pattern
Cut 1 fleece
Cut 1 Peltex

Place on fold

SNOWMAN CARD HOLDER BASKET
Full-Size Pattern
Cut 1 fleece
Cut 1 Peltex

short ends together by zigzag-stitching the center cut seam, making sure part of the stitch goes to each side of the center cut edges. Apply an even line of fabric glue around outside edges of the circular bottom piece. Carefully place bottom circle inside basket and press sides to edges of bottom.

2. Cut nose pieces from orange felt or fleece. With right sides together, sew along outside edges in a ¼-inch seam allowance, leaving straight end open for turning. Turn right side out and lightly stuff with Polyfil. Turn ends in ¼ inch and slipstitch opening closed, using matching sewing thread. Sew nose to front of basket, tacking with a few hand stitches using matching sewing thread. Using black sewing thread, sew buttons in place with nose to make snowman face.

3. Cut 4 earmuff shapes from purple fleece or felt. With right sides together, sew 2 circles together with a ¼-inch seam, leaving an opening for turning. Repeat for the other set of circles. Turn right side out and lightly stuff with Polyfil. Turn ends in ½ inch and slipstitch opening closed, using matching sewing thread. Place wrong sides of black felt strips together and zigzag stitch together along outside edges. Place handle over sides of basket and poke small holes through handle and basket sides. Slip paper fasteners through holes and secure handle in place. Attach earmuffs over ends of handle by making several hand stitches through muffs and basket, using matching sewing thread.

Paper Box Frosty
Shown on page 93

WHAT YOU NEED

4 round paper boxes: 1 large, 1 medium, 1 small, and 1 extra-small
Acrylic paints: cream, dark green, light green, orange, pink, and black
Paintbrushes in assorted sizes
Dark green felt
Double-stick tape
Crafts glue
2 pearl buttons
Black felt

WHAT YOU DO

1. Paint large, medium, and small box cream. Paint the extra-small box dark green. Let dry.

2. Remove the lid of the extra-small box and wrap with felt. Wrap the lid of the small box with felt; glue. Stack the boxes on top of each other and secure with double-stick tape. Paint the snowman face and trees on the boxes. Paint the scarf overlapping the fringe down to the bottom box.

3. Wrap a 1-inch-wide piece of black felt around the brim of the hat and glue the buttons to the snowman front.

Warm Winter Welcome
Shown on page 94

WHAT YOU NEED

Blue canning jars
Wire basket
Fresh greenery
Blue ornaments

Fresh snow
White taper candles
White acrylic snowflake

WHAT YOU DO

Arrange the jars in the wire basket. Place snow in the jars. Arrange the greenery around the jars and tuck in the snowflakes. Place the tapers in the snow in the jars. Place arrangement away from any flammable surface.

Never leave a burning candle unattended.

Let it Snow Greeting
Shown on page 95

WHAT YOU NEED

Purchased card blank in desired blue color
Rubber stamp with "Let it Snow" message
Fine white glitter
Small white buttons in three sizes
Crafts glue
Paintbrush

WHAT YOU DO

Plan stamp and button snowman placement. Stamp the card and dust with the fine white glitter. Glue the buttons in place to resemble a snowman, turning the holes in the buttons to resemble a face. Use the paintbrush to brush a line of glue for stick arms. Brush other lines of glue to resemble landscape, a top hat, and accents on the hat. Dust with glitter.

Add color and sparkle to your happy holiday
with projects and ideas that you make yourself.

A simple sparkling glass vase is filled with brightly colored bells to create

a **Jingle Bell Centerpiece**, *above.* Add a spiral lollipop to complete the

easy-to-make arrangement. Collect colorful package bows and ornaments

and combine them to make a **Bright Bow Wreath**, *opposite,* that will

add glimmer and shine wherever it greets your holiday guests.

Instructions are on pages 110–111.

shiny and bright

Use fun colors and techniques to stitch a **Bright Family of Stockings,** *opposite.* Each stocking has its own special personality. Peekaboo layering of the felt gives the unusual layers of color and decorative stitches add texture and appeal. Instructions are on pages 110–111.

Little touches of glitter on a purchased ornament make **Glittery Red Ornaments**, *left above*. These showy trims are easy to make using double-stick tape and fine glitter. Choose candy canes, stars, or other shapes to create **Christmas Motif Trims**, *below left*. Glimmering rhinestones spell out special Christmas messages on little **Comfort and Joy Pillows**, *opposite*. Instructions are on pages 112–113.

Clear glass vessels can serve as sparkling candleholders. Create **Twinkling Beaded Candles,** *below,* by choosing pretty clear glass tumblers and filling them with strands of beads and simple glittered tapers.

A string of pretty beads is all it takes to make holiday pillars into **Dress-Up Candles,** *above.* Find a new use for glass lampshades by placing candles inside and presenting them on pressed glass dishes. Surround the pieces with fresh fruit to make a stunning **Lampshade Candle,** *opposite.* Instructions are on pages 113–114.

Collect antique ornaments and showcase them in stemware to make

a simple centerpiece. Add a sprig of fresh greenery to complete the

Vintage Arrangement, *opposite.* Glass paints in the colors

of Christmas are swirled inside clear glass balls. Then the balls are

embellished with shimmering jewels and shiny ribbons to make

Painted Sparkle Trims, *above.* Instructions are on pages 114–115.

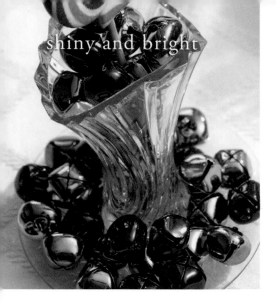

Jingle Bell Centerpiece
Shown on page 100

WHAT YOU NEED
Small clear glass vase
Small clear glass plate
Jingle bells in desired colors
Purchased lollipop

WHAT YOU DO
Be sure the glass pieces are clean and dry.
Set the vase on the plate. Fill the vase
with jingle bells. Add the lollipop in the
center of the bells. Arrange additional
bells on the plate.

Bright Bow Wreath
Shown on page 101

WHAT YOU NEED
Purchased package bows (about 30)
12-inch foam plastic wreath, such as
    Styrofoam
Small ornaments in coordinating colors
    with bows
Wire; wire cutters
Low-melt hot glue and glue gun

WHAT YOU DO
Place the wire around the wreath for a
hanger. Plan the arrangement of the bows
and ornaments as desired, overlapping
bows and ornaments. Hot-glue in place.

Bright Family of Stockings
Shown on pages 102–103

WHAT YOU NEED FOR EACH STOCKING
Tracing paper, marking pencil; scissors
Two 12×18-inch pieces felt for stocking
    body and hanging loop
Two 4×9-inch pieces contrasting felt
    for cuff
Additional assorted size felt scraps for
    embellishments on stocking fronts
8-inch strip of 1-inch-wide decorative
    ribbon (additional amount needed
    for dots on blue stocking)
Bright pink, orange, purple and teal
    blue embroidery floss
Matching sewing threads; straight pins

WHAT YOU DO
1. Enlarge and copy or trace patterns,
opposite, onto paper, also marking designs
for stocking fronts. Cut stocking body
and cuff pieces from felt. Cut a piece of
felt 1×9 inches long to be used for the
hanging loop. Place pattern onto back
side of stocking front felt piece. Beneath
the paper pattern for each design (dot,
star, strip, or zigzag), place a chunk of
desired color of felt and pin in place.
Using sewing thread the same color as

stocking body and working from the back side, machine stitch around designs, through the paper pattern. Turn stocking to the front and carefully trim away stocking front felt just inside and close to stitching lines. Embellish front designs using 6 strands of contrasting colors of embroidery floss and stitching running stitches, as desired. Running stitches may also be used to enhance the decorative ribbon used for the cuffs. Stitch ribbon to cuff front, sewing close to outside edges.

2. With right sides together, stitch stocking front to back, using ¼-inch seam allowance. Carefully clip curves, turn, and press. With right sides together, stitch side seams of cuffs. Fold hanging loop in half and place inside stocking at side edge, with top raw edges at top edge of stocking; baste in place. Insert cuff inside stocking, with right side of cuff to the wrong side of stocking and top raw edges even. Using a ¼-inch seam allowance, stitch around top to attach cuff to stocking. Turn cuff over top of stocking to outside and press.

BRIGHT FAMILY OF STOCKINGS
DOTS STOCKING
Enlarge 400%
Cut 2

BRIGHT FAMILY OF STOCKINGS
STOCKING CUFF
Enlarge 400%
Cut 2 for each stocking

BRIGHT FAMILY
OF STOCKINGS
STARS STOCKING
Enlarge 400%
Cut 2

BRIGHT FAMILY
OF STOCKINGS
STRIPES STOCKING
Enlarge 400%
Cut 2

BRIGHT FAMILY OF STOCKINGS
ZIGZAG STOCKING
Enlarge 400%
Cut 2

Comfort and Joy Pillows
Shown on page 104

WHAT YOU NEED FOR 2 PILLOWS
¼ yard *each* white and red velvet
Patterns for words
Tracing paper; pencil
2⅛ yards of ⅜-inch cording
Press cloth; iron
Assorted sizes iron-on crystals
  (approx. 170)
Tweezers
Matching sewing thread
Polyfil stuffing

WHAT YOU DO
1. Cut two 8×11-inch pieces from red velvet. Cut two 8×8-inch pieces from white velvet. Cut 1¾-inch-wide strips from red velvet to piece together to a 43-inch length. Cut 1¾-inch-wide strips from white velvet to piece together to a 35-inch length.

2. Trace words onto paper and center wording patterns on back side of pillow front fabric. Using a light box or holding up to a sunny window, use a pencil to lightly mark lines to place jewels. Place fabric front on flat ironing surface. Use tweezers to place crystals on lines of letters. Carefully place press cloth over crystals and iron in place, following manufacturer's directions.

3. Cover cording by wrapping wrong sides of velvet strips over cording and machine stitching close to cording using a zipper foot. Baste cording to pillow front, clipping cording at corners. With right sides together, machine sew front to back, using a ½-inch seam allowance and leaving a 4-inch opening for turning. Clip corners and turn right side out. Stuff lightly with polyfil stuffing and hand stitch remaining seam opening closed.

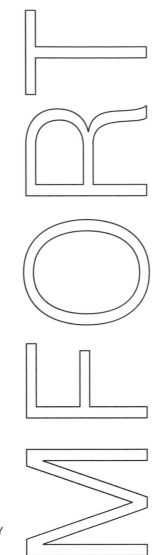

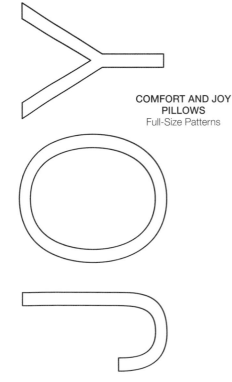

**COMFORT AND JOY
PILLOWS**
Full-Size Patterns

Glittery Red Ornaments
Shown on page 105

WHAT YOU NEED
Purchased red matte glass ornaments
Scissors
Double stick tape; fine red glitter

WHAT YOU DO
Cut small pieces of double-stick tape and adhere to the ornament. See Photo A. Carefully peel back one side of the tape, leaving the sticky surface. See Photo B. Sprinkle glitter on the surface. See Photo C. Shake off excess.

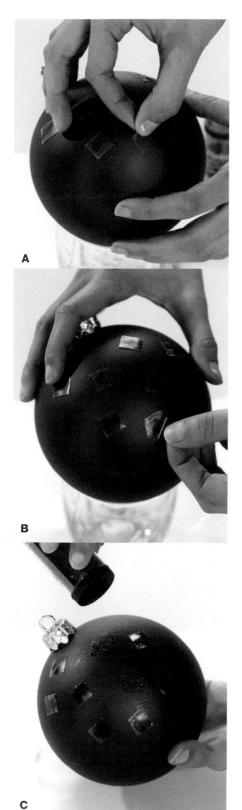

A

B

C

on the ornament. Dust with red glitter. Let dry. Using the crafts glue, make dots between the glitter dots. Dust with light pink or white glitter. Allow to dry.

2. For the star motifs, place a dot of glue on the ornament and, using a toothpick, spread the glue into a star shape. Sprinkle with glitter. Repeat for other stars. Allow to dry.

Christmas Motif Trims

Shown on page 105

WHAT YOU NEED

Purchased white or black ornament
Crafts glue; toothpick
Red, pink, and white fine glitter

WHAT YOU DO

1. For the candy cane motifs, make dots of glue, leaving a space between each dot

Twinkling Beaded Candles

Shown on page 106

WHAT YOU NEED

Two glass tumblers
String of bead garland in desired color
Two taper candles
Glass plate or tray
Ornaments to match color of bead garland

WHAT YOU DO

Place a taper in each tumbler. Arrange the beaded garland around each candle in the tumblers. Readjust candle to straighten if necessary. Set tumblers on glass tray. Arrange ornaments around the tumblers.

1 medium green 4-inch pillar candle
24-gauge wire
Pearl-style beads
Long red cylinder beads
Straight pins

WHAT YOU DO
Measure the diameter of each candle. Cut a piece of wire 8 inches longer than the measurement of each of the candles. Make a loop at the end of the wire and begin stringing the pearl beads and the cylinder beads alternately. Bend the beaded wire to form curves that resemble drips from a candle. Twist the ends of the wires together and place over the candle. Secure in the back if necessary with straight pins.

Lampshade Candle

Shown on page 107

WHAT YOU NEED
Glass lampshade (available at
    home centers)
Votive candle in desired colors

Dressed-Up Candles

Shown on page 106

WHAT YOU NEED
Measuring tape
1 light green 7-inch pillar candle

Glass plate
Fruits such as star fruit, limes,
    cranberries, and oranges
Knife

WHAT YOU DO
Place lampshade upside down on plate. Place votive in the center of the lampshade. Use the knife to cut thin slices of fruit. Arrange around the candle.

Vintage Arrangement

Shown on page 108

WHAT YOU NEED
Vintage stemware
Vintage Christmas ornaments
Sprigs of fresh greenery

WHAT YOU DO
Be sure the glasses are clean and dry. Place the ornaments in the glasses, arranging 3 or more in each glass. Add the sprigs of greenery. Set in a row on the table for a centerpiece.

A

B

C

D

Painted Sparkle Trims
Shown on page 109

WHAT YOU NEED
Clear glass balls with removable tops
   (available at crafts stores)
3 colors of paint suitable for glass
Tumbler
Small pieces of narrow ribbon
Self-stick jewels
Crafts glue suitable for glass

WHAT YOU DO
1. Remove the top from the glass ball.
Place a few drops of one color of glass
paint inside the ball. Rotate the ball to
move the paint. Add another color of
paint. See Photo A. Swirl that with the
first color. Add a third color of paint.
See Photo B. Swirl the paint again and
set in tumbler. See Photo C. Move the
ball in the tumbler to various positions
during the next hour so paint swirls and
combines. When the paint is dry, replace
the top.
2. Tie small bows using the narrow
ribbon. Decorate the ornaments by gluing
pieces of ribbon and small bows to the
surface as desired. Allow to dry. Add
stick-on jewels if desired. See Photo D.

christmas morning brunch

With make-ahead ease, these tasty recipes inspire delightful midmorning get-togethers.

Fill your kitchen with the fragrant aroma of warm spices in **Festive Maple-Butter Twists,** *opposite.* Freshly brewed **Simply Spiced Coffee,** *above,* goes together as quick as a wink. Recipes are on pages 123–124.

Let scrumptious **Ham Soufflé Roll**, *above,* be the focal point of your

brunch. Serve hearty offerings, such as **Maple-Mustard Sausages**

and **Cottage-Fried New Potatoes**, *opposite,* alongside. Presenting

the food in bold red and white serving pieces sets the holiday mood.

Recipes are on pages 124–125.

A sweet surprise of **Minty White Chocolate Nog**, *right,* is a fun new twist on classic eggnog. **Stuffed French Toast**, *below,* bakes in easy-to-serve stacks after chilling overnight. Recipes are on pages 125–126.

Add color and crunch to brunch with **Broccoli, Cheddar, and Bacon Medley**, *above*. Even kids love this! Recipe on page 126.

Tender, moist **Pear-Almond Muffins,** *above,* are even more delicious the day after baking. Kick off brunch on a flavorful note with **Minted Fruit Slush,** *right.* Or serve the icy refresher between courses. Recipes are on page 127.

Festive Maple-Butter Twists

Shown on page 116

WHAT YOU NEED

- ⅔ cup milk
- 2 eggs
- ⅓ cup butter, cut up
- ¼ cup water
- 4 cups bread flour
- ¼ cup granulated sugar
- 1½ teaspoons salt
- 2½ teaspoons active dry yeast or bread machine yeast
- ½ cup packed brown sugar
- ⅓ cup granulated sugar
- ¼ cup all-purpose flour
- ¼ cup butter, softened
- ¼ cup pure maple syrup or maple-flavored syrup
- 1 teaspoon ground cinnamon
- ½ teaspoon maple flavoring
- ½ cup chopped pecans

WHAT YOU DO

1. Add the first eight ingredients to bread machine according to the manufacturer's directions. Select the dough cycle. When cycle is complete, remove dough. Punch down. Cover and let rest for 10 minutes.

2. Meanwhile, for filling, in a small bowl stir together brown sugar, the ⅓ cup granulated sugar, all-purpose flour, ¼ cup butter, the maple syrup, cinnamon, and maple flavoring; set aside. Grease two 8×1½-inch round baking pans. Grease outsides of two 6-ounce custard cups. Place a cup upside down in center of each greased pan; set aside.

3. Divide dough in half. On a lightly floured surface, roll one portion to a 16×6-inch rectangle. Spread with half the filling; sprinkle with half the pecans. Starting from a long side, roll up in a spiral; seal edge and ends. Cut spiral in half lengthwise. See Photo A, *below*.

4. To shape, line up the halves side by side with cut sides up; loosely twist halves together, keeping cut sides up. See Photo B, *below*. Gently stretch to 20 inches long. Transfer to prepared baking pan, forming twist in a ring around custard cup. See Photo C, *below*. Moisten ends and press together to seal. Repeat with remaining dough, filling, and pecans. Cover and let rise in a warm place until nearly double (30 to 40 minutes).

5. Preheat oven to 350°F. Place baking pans on baking sheets to catch any drips while baking. Bake about 25 minutes or until golden brown. Cool in pans on wire racks for 5 minutes. Loosen edges and carefully remove cups. Remove bread from pans; cool slightly on wire racks. Serve warm or cool completely. Makes 16 servings.

Make-Ahead Directions: Prepare as directed. Wrap each bread twist in foil or plastic wrap; store in a cool, dry place (not in the refrigerator) for 2 to 3 days. For longer storage, place each completely cooled bread twist in a freezer bag or an airtight container or wrap in heavy foil. Freeze up to 3 months. Thaw at room temperature for 1 hour.

A

B

C

Simply Spiced Coffee

Shown on page 117

WHAT YOU NEED

- 4 cups brewed coffee
- 2 inches stick cinnamon
- ½ teaspoon whole allspice
- 2 2×½-inch strips orange peel
  Stick cinnamon (optional)
  Orange peel strips (optional)

WHAT YOU DO

1. In a medium saucepan combine coffee, 2 inches stick cinnamon, allspice, and orange peel. Bring to boiling; reduce heat. Cover and simmer for 5 minutes.
2. Remove cinnamon, allspice, and orange peel from coffee with a slotted spoon. Pour coffee into cups. If desired, garnish with cinnamon sticks and orange peel strips. Makes 6 (5-ounce) servings.

Ham Soufflé Roll

This twice-baked egg roll first bakes as a soufflé in a shallow pan before it is rolled and chilled. Allow 45 minutes of oven time to heat it through on the day of your brunch. Shown on page 118.

WHAT YOU NEED

- ¼ cup butter
- ½ cup all-purpose flour
- ⅛ teaspoon ground black pepper
- 2 cups milk
- 6 egg yolks, lightly beaten
- 6 egg whites
- ¼ teaspoon cream of tartar
- 6 ounces thinly sliced cooked ham
- 6 ounces thinly sliced provolone or Swiss cheese
- 1 recipe Parsley Sauce
  Snipped fresh parsley (optional)

WHAT YOU DO

1. Preheat oven to 375°F. Line a 15×10×1-inch baking pan with foil, extending foil about 1 inch over edges of pan. Grease and lightly flour foil; set pan aside.
2. In a medium saucepan melt butter over medium heat. Stir in flour and pepper. Gradually stir in the milk. Cook and stir until mixture is thickened and bubbly. Cool mixture slightly. Place egg yolks in a medium bowl; gradually stir in milk mixture.
3. In a large mixing bowl combine egg whites and cream of tartar. Beat with an electric mixer until stiff peaks form (tips stand straight). Fold some of the beaten egg whites into the egg yolk mixture. Fold egg yolk mixture into the remaining beaten egg whites. Spread in the prepared baking pan.
4. Bake about 20 minutes or until soufflé is puffed and a knife inserted in center comes out clean.
5. Meanwhile, place a long sheet of heavy foil (about 22×18 inches) on a large baking sheet. Generously grease the foil. Immediately loosen edges of soufflé from baking pan. Invert soufflé onto the

foil-lined baking sheet. Carefully peel off foil.
6. Place ham and cheese slices in single layers on soufflé. Starting from a short side, use foil on baking sheet to lift and help roll soufflé, removing foil as you roll. Use foil to lift soufflé roll into a 13×9×2-inch baking pan. Fold the foil over the soufflé roll to cover. Chill soufflé roll for 2 to 24 hours. Prepare Parsley Sauce; cover and chill up to 24 hours.
7. Preheat oven to 350°F. Bake soufflé roll, covered with the foil, about 45 minutes or until heated through. Meanwhile, shake sauce; transfer to a medium saucepan. Cook and stir over medium heat until thickened and bubbly. Cook and stir for 2 minutes more.
8. To serve, uncover soufflé roll. Use the foil to lift soufflé roll from pan. Using two large spatulas, transfer soufflé roll to a warm serving platter (or use foil to roll soufflé onto platter). If desired, spoon a little sauce on soufflé roll. Slice with a serrated knife and serve with the remaining sauce. If desired, garnish with snipped parsley. Makes 8 servings.
Parsley Sauce: In a blender or food processor combine ½ cup lightly packed fresh parsley sprigs; 2 green onions, cut up; and 1 teaspoon dried basil, crushed. Cover and blend or process until finely chopped. Add 1½ cups whipping cream, 1 tablespoon cornstarch, 1 tablespoon Dijon-style mustard, and ¼ teaspoon salt. Cover and blend or process for 10 to

more or until potatoes are tender and browned, turning frequently. Makes 8 servings.

Make-Ahead Directions: Transfer all the cooked potato mixture to a 2-quart baking dish or casserole. Cover with foil. Hold in a 200°F oven up to 1 hour.

20 seconds or until mixture is slightly thickened. (Do not overblend.) Transfer mixture to a screw-top jar.

Maple-Mustard Sausages

Shown on page 119

WHAT YOU NEED

- 2 12-ounce packages (24 links total) breakfast sausages
- ¼ cup packed brown sugar
- ¼ cup pure maple syrup
- 2 teaspoons dry mustard

WHAT YOU DO

1. In an extra large skillet cook sausages according to package directions. Drain fat from skillet.

2. Meanwhile, in a small bowl stir together sugar, syrup, and mustard; add mixture to skillet with sausages. Cook, uncovered, over medium heat for 3 to 4 minutes or until sausages are glazed, stirring frequently. Serve immediately. Makes 8 to 12 servings.

Cottage-Fried New Potatoes

If you're short on skillets, cook the potatoes in batches and keep the first batch warm in a 200°F oven while cooking the second batch. Shown on page 119.

WHAT YOU NEED

- 6 tablespoons butter
- 2 pounds tiny new potatoes, cut into wedges
- ½ teaspoon salt
- ¼ teaspoon garlic powder
- ¼ teaspoon black pepper
- 1 large onion, chopped
- 1 medium red sweet pepper, chopped

WHAT YOU DO

1. In two large skillets divide and melt butter. (If necessary, add additional butter during cooking.) Place half the potatoes in each skillet; sprinkle with half the salt, garlic powder, and black pepper. Cook, covered, over medium heat for 8 minutes. Add half the onion and sweet pepper to each. Cook, uncovered, 8 to 10 minutes

Minty White Chocolate Nog

Dress up this easy eggnog fix-up for the holidays, using peppermint sticks to stir the drink. Shown on page 120.

WHAT YOU NEED

- 1 quart purchased eggnog
- 1 cup chopped white baking chocolate
- ⅓ cup crushed peppermint sticks
  Freshly grated nutmeg
  Peppermint sticks

WHAT YOU DO

1. In a medium saucepan combine eggnog, white baking chocolate, and crushed peppermint. Cook and stir over low heat until chocolate is melted and mixture is heated through.

2. Serve drink warm topped with freshly grated nutmeg and additional peppermint sticks as stirrers. Makes 8 to 10 (3- to 5-ounce) servings.

Broccoli, Cheddar, and Bacon Medley
Shown on page 121

Stuffed French Toast
The cream cheese and fruit filling makes this breakfast favorite an extra-special treat. Shown on page 120.

WHAT YOU NEED
- 8 ¾-inch-thick slices French bread*
- 1 recipe Cream Cheese Filling
- 4 eggs
- 1 cup milk
- 1 cup orange juice
   Powdered sugar
   Maple syrup

WHAT YOU DO

1. In a 3-quart rectangular baking dish arrange half the bread slices. Top each slice with some of the Cream Cheese Filling. Add remaining bread slices.

2. In a medium bowl beat together eggs, milk, and orange juice. Slowly pour egg mixture over bread slices, covering all the bread. Cover and chill for 2 to 24 hours.

3. Preheat oven to 375°F. Line a 15×10×1-inch baking pan with parchment paper or nonstick foil. Arrange bread stacks in pan. Bake, uncovered, for 30 to 35 minutes or until golden, turning halfway through baking. Sprinkle with powdered sugar. Serve with maple syrup. Makes 4 servings.

Cream Cheese Filling: In a medium bowl combine one 8-ounce package cream cheese, ½ cup chopped dried apricots or golden raisins, and 1 teaspoon ground cinnamon.

*Test Kitchen Tip: Depending on the diameter of the bread, you may need to vary the number of slices of bread to fill the dish.

WHAT YOU NEED
- 4 cups broccoli florets
- 1 small red onion, chopped or cut into thin wedges (½ cup)
- 1 cup cubed cheddar or smoked cheddar cheese (4 ounces)
- 5 slices bacon, crisp-cooked, drained, and crumbled
- ½ cup mayonnaise or light mayonnaise dressing
- ¼ cup bottled coleslaw or buttermilk ranch salad dressing
- 2 tablespoons vinegar
- 1 tablespoon sugar

WHAT YOU DO

1. In a large bowl combine broccoli, onion, cheese, and bacon.

2. For dressing, in a small bowl stir together mayonnaise, coleslaw dressing, vinegar, and sugar. Pour dressing over broccoli mixture; toss to coat. Makes 6 side-dish servings.

Make-Ahead Directions: Cut up the broccoli, chop the onion, cube the cheese, combine the dressing ingredients, and chill each in separate containers overnight. Just before serving, cook the bacon and toss the salad together.

Pear-Almond Muffins

Ginger- and honey-laced cream cheese complements the golden muffins. Sprinkle the almonds on top just before baking for toasted flavor. Shown on page 122.

WHAT YOU NEED

    Nonstick cooking spray
- 1 cup all-purpose flour
- ½ cup packed brown sugar
- 2 teaspoons baking powder
- ½ teaspoon ground ginger
- ¼ teaspoon salt
- ¾ cup whole bran cereal
- ¾ cup fat-free milk
- ¾ cup chopped, peeled pear
- 2 egg whites, lightly beaten
- 3 tablespoons canola oil
- 2 tablespoons sliced almonds
- 1 recipe Ginger-Cream Spread

WHAT YOU DO

1. Preheat oven to 400°F. Lightly coat twelve 2½-inch muffin cups with nonstick cooking spray or line with paper bake cups; set aside. In a large bowl stir together flour, brown sugar, baking powder, ginger, and salt. Make a well in the center of the flour mixture; set aside.
2. In a medium bowl stir together cereal and milk; let mixture stand for 5 minutes. Stir in pear, egg whites, and oil. Add cereal mixture all at once to flour mixture; stir just until moistened (batter should be lumpy).
3. Spoon batter into prepared muffin cups, filling each three-fourths full. Sprinkle with almonds. Bake for 15 to 18 minutes or until a toothpick inserted near centers comes out clean.
4. Cool in muffin cups on a wire rack for 5 minutes. Remove muffins from muffin cups. Serve warm with Ginger-Cream Spread. Makes 12 muffins.

Ginger-Cream Spread: In a small bowl stir together half of an 8-ounce tub light cream cheese, 2 teaspoons finely chopped crystallized ginger or ¼ teaspoon ground ginger, and 2 teaspoons honey.

Make-Ahead Directions: Prepare and bake the muffins; cool. Place in an airtight container. Cover and freeze up to 3 months. Thaw muffins, covered, at room temperature. Wrap muffins in foil and warm in a 350°F oven about 10 minutes or until heated through. Prepare Ginger-Cream Spread as directed; cover and chill up to 3 days.

Minted Fruit Slush

Shown on page 122

WHAT YOU NEED

- ½ cup sugar
- 16 fresh mint leaves
- ½ of a 12-ounce can frozen limeade concentrate
- ½ cup ginger ale or sparkling water with lime flavor
- 2 teaspoons finely shredded lime peel
- 5 cups frozen unsweetened mixed berries, thawed slightly (20 ounces)
- 1 mango, seeded, peeled, and chopped
- 1 cup chopped fresh pineapple
    Additional mint leaves (optional)

WHAT YOU DO

1. In a large saucepan bring ¾ cup *water* and sugar just to boiling, stirring to dissolve sugar. Remove from heat; add half the mint leaves. Using a large spoon, press leaves on the side of the pan to bruise slightly. Let stand 10 minutes.
2. Remove mint leaves; discard. Finely snip remaining mint leaves. Add to sugar mixture along with limeade concentrate, ginger ale, and lime peel. Stir in berries, mango, and pineapple. Cover; freeze at least 8 hours or until completely frozen. To serve, let fruit mixture stand at room temperature for 10 minutes. Scrape mixture into slush and spoon into serving cups. If desired, garnish with additional mint leaves. Makes 8 to 12 servings.

Embrace your creative spirit this holiday by finding new uses for some old favorites.

festively frugal
and fun

Keep your old sweaters or purchase some at a used clothing store to make a

Felted Wool Wreath Pin and **Geometric Pot Holders**, *above* and *opposite*.

Both of these clever gifts were made from a well-worn green

wool sweater. The little pin is made from tiny squares

of the felted sweater. The handsome potholders use

two layers of felted fabric with a blanket-stitch trim.

Instructions are on page 140.

Castaway shirts were cut apart and stitched for colorful **Printed Luggage Tags,** *opposite.* These original, personalized tags make it easy to locate ho-hum luggage and are quick to make. Recycle glass jars into pretty **Beaded Candy Cane Jars,** *left,* to hold all kinds of holiday goodies. Beads and wire combine to make the sparkling trim. Instructions are on pages 141–142.

A favorite but well-worn angora sweater and scraps

of lace take on new life as **Winter White Accessories**,

opposite and *above*. One sweater can make a cozy muff, a sweet purse,

and a warm scarf. The pieces are trimmed with simple lace and tiny bows.

Instructions are on pages 142–143.

Last year's Christmas cards can become stunning **Christmas Card Ornaments,** *above* and *right,* using a simple pattern and a touch of glitter. Instructions are on page 143.

Combine department or specialty store
shopping bags and fronts of holiday cards to
make **Holiday Gift Bags**, *above*. The store name
is disguised with the pretty card image. Instructions are on page 144.

With scraps of soft fabric and snippets of ribbon, you can create

Baby's Favorite Blanket, *above*. The little touchable treasure combines

pieces of satin, fleece, terry cloth, and other fabric favorites with ribbons

that little fingers love to hold. Instructions are on page 144.

Perfect blooms are created from cut-and-coil circles of felted sweaters. The little flowers are assembled into a lovely **Holiday Blooms Wreath,** *below*. Instructions are on page 145.

Here is one route that you'll love. Gather outdated or tattered maps and use them for clever **Map Wraps,** *above.* Add some ribbon trims to match the colors of the maps. This year, instead of making big fluffy bows, use just a little ribbon by trimming your gifts with simple **Button Trimmed Packages,** *opposite.* Instructions are on page 145.

Felted Wool Wreath Pin

Shown on page 128

WHAT YOU NEED

Discarded wool sweater
Matching thread; needle
Assorted beads, ribbons, trims
¼-inch-wide grosgrain ribbon
Gold metallic balls from a floral stem
Safety pin or purchased jewelry pin
    backing
Fabric glue

WHAT YOU DO

1. Felt a wool sweater. For felting
instructions, see page 158. Cut forty
1-inch squares. Using a double thread in
matching color, stitch squares together
in a long string by inserting the needle
into the center of each square to thread
them all together. See Photos A and B.

A

2. Circle ends together and tack in
place with a couple of securing stitches.
Decorate wreath with desired trims,
stitching or gluing in place. Attach
pin to back by sewing in place with
matching thread.

Geometric Pot Holders

Shown on page 129

WHAT YOU NEED

Discarded wool sweater
Tracing paper or copier; pencil
¼ yard heat resistant fleece, such as
    Thermolam
Coordinating yarn

WHAT YOU DO

1. Felt sweater. For felting instructions
see page 158.
2. Enlarge and trace or copy desired
patterns, *opposite*, onto tracing paper.
For each pot holder, cut two pattern
pieces from wool sweater and one from
heat-resistant fleece. Place wrong sides
of pot holder pieces together.
3. Trim fleece ¼ inch smaller than
sweater pieces and beneath circle cutout.
Place fleece between sweater pieces. Pin
layers together.
4. Work buttonhole stitch around outside
edges and around inside of circle opening,
using coordinating yarn. Steam press pot
holder to reshape edges after sewing.

B

Printed Luggage Tags

Shown on page 130

WHAT YOU NEED FOR EACH TAG

Tracing paper; pencil
Two 3½×5½-inch pieces of discarded
    shirting fabric *Note:* Shirt placket
    or front buttoned openings make
    interesting details to incorporate on
    tag back pieces
One 3½×5½-inch piece of double
    fusible Peltex stabilizer
Sewing thread
½ yard of ½-inch-wide grosgrain ribbon
Pinking shears; scissors; pins
2⅞×4 inch piece of clear plastic
    (recycled report covers, financial,
    or business folders work well)

WHAT YOU DO

1. Trace desired pattern, *right* and *below*, and cut out. Set aside. Following manufacturer's directions, fuse Peltex between 2 layers of fabric, with right sides of fabric out. Trace luggage tag pattern onto paper and cut out. Pin pattern onto reinforced fabric and cut out using pinking shears. Lay plastic on top of one side of fabric tag, with lower squared edges even.

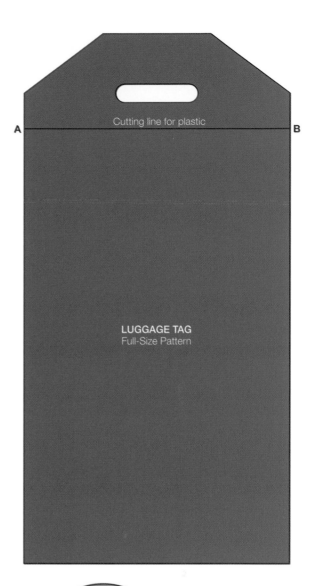

Cutting line for plastic

A   B

LUGGAGE TAG
Full-Size Pattern

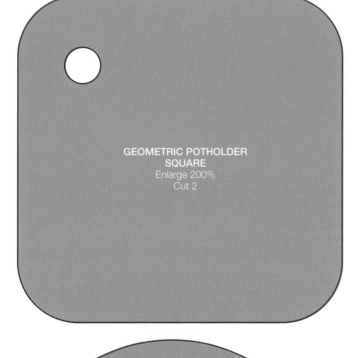

GEOMETRIC POTHOLDER
SQUARE
Enlarge 200%
Cut 2

GEOMETRIC POTHOLDER
CIRCLE
Enlarge 200%
Cut 2

GEOMETRIC POTHOLDER
TRIANGLE
Enlarge 200%
Cut 2

2. Sew close to cut edges through all thicknesses, starting from point A, around outside and bottom edge, up opposite side, to point B, backstitching at beginning and end. Cut out oval from pattern and place pattern on fabric tag. With marking pen, trace oval shape onto fabric. With sharp point of scissors, cut out oval opening. Reinforce edges of opening by zigzag stitching around edges.

3. Diagonally cut ribbon ends. Fold ribbon in half and place length along center back of tag, marking a pin about 4 inches from the fold. Stitch tag around remaining unsewn top edges, starting and stopping at points A and B and backstitching at top over ribbon. Insert business card or make a 2×3½-inch cardboard identification tag. Tie ribbon ends into a loose decorative knot at the back of the tag.

4. To attach to luggage handle, place ribbon loop over handle, reach through loop and pull tag bottom through loop. Pull ribbon snuggly to secure.

Note: Use each family member's discarded clothing and matching ribbons to readily identify items.

Beaded Candy Cane Jars

Shown on page 131

WHAT YOU NEED

28 inches of 16-gauge copper wire
Round-nose pliers

1 10- to 12-ounce jar
8 inches of 18-gauge copper wire (for candy cane)
9 red and 8 clear 6mm bicone beads (or other red/clear bead combination to total 4½ inches)
Other embellishment supplies:
    Small pieces of 18-gauge copper wire, "Wish" charm, other charms, assorted red, clear, and silver beads
Note: *Before starting, make sure the holes in the beads are large enough to accommodate the 18-gauge wire.*

WHAT YOU DO

1. Center wire on neck of the jar and wrap around so ends meet. Cross the wire and wrap in the opposite direction. Pull tightly and twist to hold in place.

2. Using round-nose pliers, bend ends into loops and curls for hanging embellishments.

3. To make candy cane embellishement, with round-nose pliers, grasp the end of the 18-gauge wire and curl it around the tip of the pliers to make a loop. Add alternating red and clear beads to the wire until there are approximately 4½ inches of beads. End the wire with another loop. Bend to make the curve of the candy cane. Make an S-shape connector with wire and use it to hang "Wish" charm on the loop of the candy cane. Make an O-ring with the wire large enough to fit around the cane and hang it on a loop on the jar.

4. Use round-nose pliers to create loops of wire to hang other embellishments. Add beads to the wire and finish with loops, twists, and cork-screw shapes as desired.

Winter White Accessories

Shown on pages 132–133

WHAT YOU NEED
For all projects:
Discarded angora sweater
Matching thread
For Scarf:
Scraps of antique lace
For Muff:
Medium-weight interfacing
    (19×14-inch piece)
Matching thread

Scraps of lace
11×15-inch piece of faux fur
16-inch length of ¼-inch decorative cording
For Purse:
51-inch length of ¼-inch decorative cording
Matching embroidery floss

WHAT YOU DO FOR ALL PROJECTS
Felt sweater. See page 158 for felting tips.

For Scarf:

1. Cut sleeves from preshrunk sweater, cutting open along underarm seam. Press flat. Cut lengths about 5¼ inches wide and the length of the sleeves, leaving ribbing intact at bottom edge of sleeves. Narrowly hem side edges of lace for bottom edges of scarf.

2. Place lace just under the ribbing edges and stitch in place on each scarf piece.

Join 2 scarf pieces by stitching lace between sections, overlapping lace on top of cut sweater edges. Straight stitch or zigzag stitch lace to sweater pieces. From scraps, cut 2 lengths of sweater fabric, ½×9 inches long. Tie lengths into small bows and tack to center of ends of scarf.

For Muff:

1. Cut sweater body to make a rectangular 19×14-inch piece with ribbing from the bottom sweater edge at the 14-inch side (rectangle may need to be pieced together from 2 small pieces of fabric). Sew lace across bottom, just above the ribbing edge. Iron medium-weight interfacing to back of sweater fabric to give a little extra body or to stabilize any stretchiness. With wrong sides together overlap ribbing edge over bottom edge of rectangle to make a tube that, when flattened out, measures 7½×14 inches. Baste across overlapped section at side edges.

2. Sew fur by bringing shorter edges together and folding in half to make a 11×7½-inch piece. Sew with right sides together in a ½-inch seam across the 11-inch length to make a tube. Turn fur right side out.

3. Slip fur inside sweater tube, with right sides together. At top right side of sweater tube, insert decorative cording, folding length in half so ends are caught in seam and loop is inside between layers. Sew fur to sweater, using ½-inch seam allowance to sew around the right side circle.

4. Align remaining circular edges, sewing together in a ½-inch seam. Turn sweater right side out by reaching through the turned-over ribbing edge. The top sweater piece at the side edges will roll about 1 inch to the inside fur. From sweater scraps, cut a ¾×12-inch strip and tie into a bow. Tack to the center of the lace on finished muff.

For Purse:

1. Cut scrap of sweater to 6×11-inches, with finished ribbing edge at the 6-inch side. With wrong sides together, fold bottom edge up and ribbing edge over to form a flap, making a 5×6-inch shape. Place cording between layers at side edges, extending from bottom edge to top fold. Sew with a 3-step zigzag stitch or

other stitch with width so stitching is over cording and through both layers of sweater at side edges.

2. To make buttonhole on flap, cut a small slit through the flap layer of sweater fabric at the center. Using 2 strands matching embroidery floss, stitch around the cut slit using the buttonhole stitch to reinforce. Sew decorative button underneath slit onto the front flap of the purse.

3. From sweater fabric scraps, cut a 1½×6-inch strip. With wrong sides together, zigzag long edges together to make a ½-inch cording. Tie a loose knot in the center, overlap ends, and machine sew over ends to the bottom section of the purse, just under the buttonhole.

Christmas Card Ornaments

Shown on page 134

WHAT YOU NEED

Tracing paper; pencil
Scrap of cardboard
Christmas cards to recycle
Crafts glue
Extra-fine glitter
9-inch length of fine metallic cording
for each ornament

WHAT YOU DO

1. Trace or copy circle pattern, *below*, onto tracing paper and cut out. Trace circle pattern onto cardboard piece and cut out. Trace around cardboard circle onto Christmas cards, making 6 circles for each ornament.

2. Cut out circles and fold each in half with the colorful side folded to the inside. Spread crafts glue onto the backside of 1 half circle. Press back side of another circle to this to glue 2 circles together. Continue gluing several circles together.

3. Fold cording in half, add a dot of glue to cut ends, and place between folds of 2 circles already glued together. Glue rest of circles together until all 6 are used to form a circle, with the folds meeting together at the center. Carefully trim around the outside circle edges so the 2 halves match up exactly.

4. Place a thin line of white glue along circle edges. Sprinkle a line of glue onto a scrap card backing piece and gently roll the outside edges through the glitter.

CHRISTMAS CARD ORNAMENT
Full-Size Pattern

festively frugal and fun

Holiday Gift Bags

Shown on page 135

WHAT YOU NEED

Christmas cards to recycle
Specialty or department store
    shopping bags
Scissors; crafts glue

Ribbon
Sticker (optional); glitter (optional)

WHAT YOU DO

Choose a card that is large enough to cover the store name on the bag. Cut the front from the card as desired and glue over the store name. Run a line of glue around the edge of the card. Starting at the top center of the card, leave 8 inches of a ribbon tail and glue the ribbon around the card. Leave another tail at the end and tie a bow at the top. Add glitter and a sticker if desired.

Baby's Favorite Blanket

Shown on page 136

WHAT YOU NEED

Tracing paper or copier; pencil
Scraps of assorted textured fabrics for
    appliqué shapes (satin, fur, terry cloth)
Four 5½-inch squares of textured pink
    fabrics (satin, fleece, plush)
Scraps of fusible webbing
10½-inch square of soft fabric for backing
5-inch-long scraps of assorted
    ribbons, laces, and rickrack
    trims (approximately 10 per side,
    depending on width of trim)
Matching sewing thread

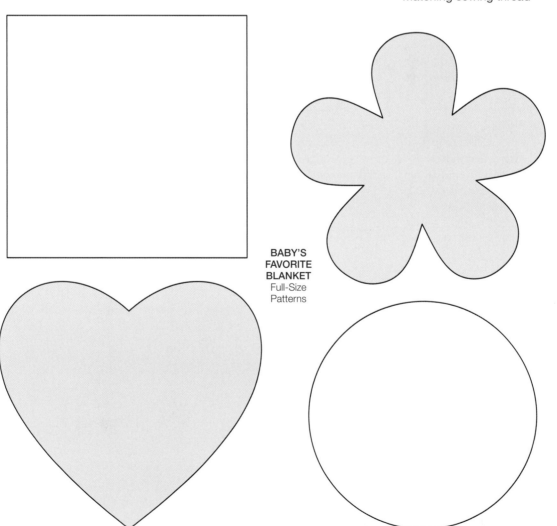

**BABY'S
FAVORITE
BLANKET**
Full-Size
Patterns

WHAT YOU DO

1. Trace or copy appliqué shapes, *opposite*, onto fusible webbing paper and fuse to the back of appliqué fabrics. Cut out shapes and fuse to the center of each of the 5½-inch squares. Machine zigzag stitch around appliqué shapes and securely stitch small ribbon bow to center of flower shape. With right sides together and using a ¼-inch seam, stitch 4 blocks together for the blanket front.
2. Fold ribbons in half and pin to right side of blanket backing fabric, having ribbon ends even with outside cut edges and loops extending toward center of fabric. Baste ribbons to outside edges of backing fabric. Place right sides of blanket front and back together and stitch in ¼-inch seam line, leaving 4 inches along one side for turning. Clip corners diagonally, turn, and lightly press. Hand stitch opening closed.

Holiday Blooms Wreath
Shown on page 137

WHAT YOU NEED
Tracing paper; pencil
100-percent-wool sweaters (about 3 to 4 sweaters) in assorted shades of red, orange, and pink
Template plastic
Crafts glue
8-inch-diameter rounded-edge green plastic-foam wreath
Straight pins
Pencil with eraser
1 yard of 2-inch-wide red ribbon

WHAT YOU DO

1. Felt the sweaters. Place the wool sweaters in the washing machine separating colors. Fill the machine with hot water and regular detergent. Agitate the fabric on the longest wash cycle and rinse in hot water. Place the sweaters in the dryer for 30 minutes. For more tips on felting, see page 158.
2. To create the roses, trace or copy the circle pattern, *below*, onto tracing paper and cut out. Trace the pattern onto template plastic and cut out. *Note:* **Do not cut pattern along the coil lines.** Cut about 120 circles from the felted sweaters. Referring to the pattern, cut each wool circle into a spiral. Starting at the outside edge at the X, roll the spiral into a rose shape, gluing the rolled spiral at the base.
3. To attach the roses, start on the inside edge and place roses close together, covering the wreath with roses by gluing them down first and then securing them with straight pins. Use the eraser end of a pencil to push each straight pin into the center of a rose to conceal the pinhead.
4. Wrap the red ribbon around the wreath and tie it in a bow.

Map Wraps
Shown on page 138

WHAT YOU NEED
Discarded maps
Package to wrap
Ribbons, trims, and stickers

WHAT YOU DO
Unfold a map and wrap a package, placing the most interesting part of the map on the package front. Embellish the package with ribbons, trims, and stickers.

Button Trimmed Packages
Shown on page 139

WHAT YOU NEED
Wrapped package
Small pieces of ribbon
Small white buttons
Crafts glue or transparent tape

WHAT YOU DO
Choose desired wrapped package. Cut the small pieces of ribbon to fit around the box. Glue or tape in place on back of box. Glue the buttons in a row on top of the ribbon.

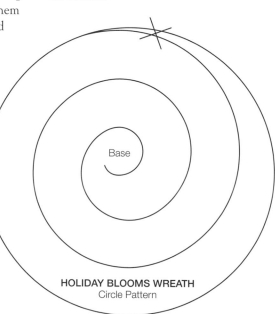

Base

HOLIDAY BLOOMS WREATH
Circle Pattern

holiday stars

This holiday, find a way to use the most blessed symbol of Christmas—the star.

A galaxy of stars creates a beautiful **Golden Table Runner**, *above* and *opposite*, to grace your holiday table. Individual stars are layered with gold print fabrics, quilted, and then combined into the interesting piece. Instructions are on page 154.

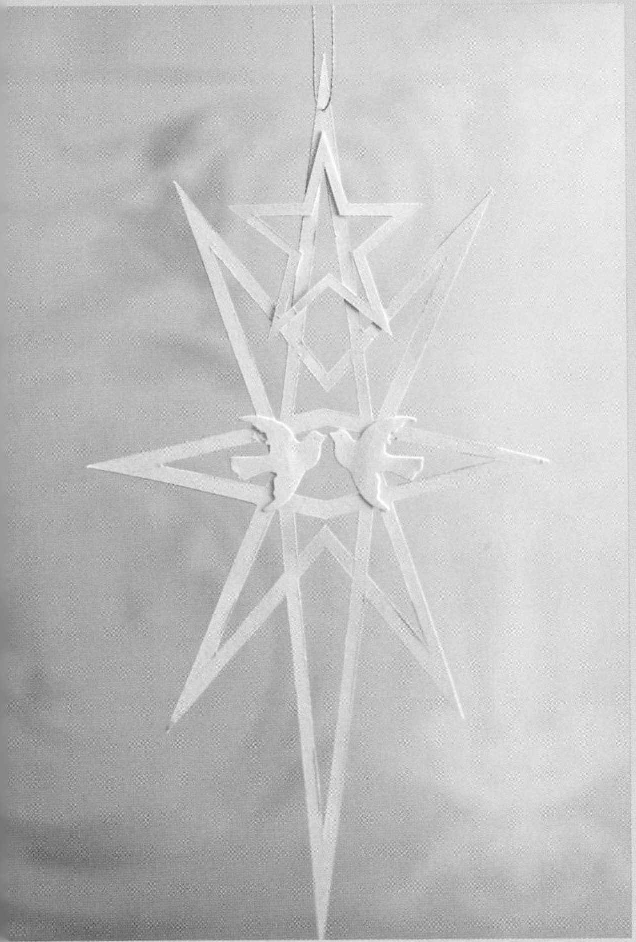

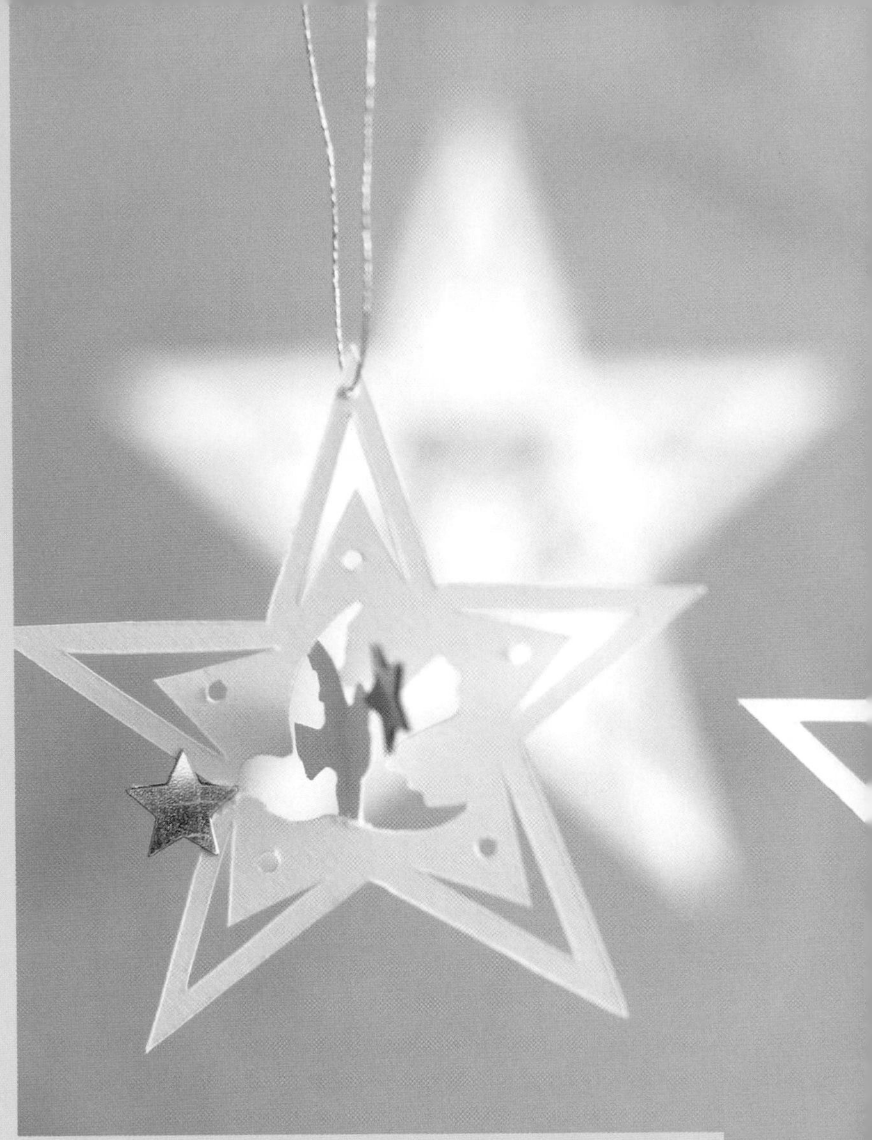

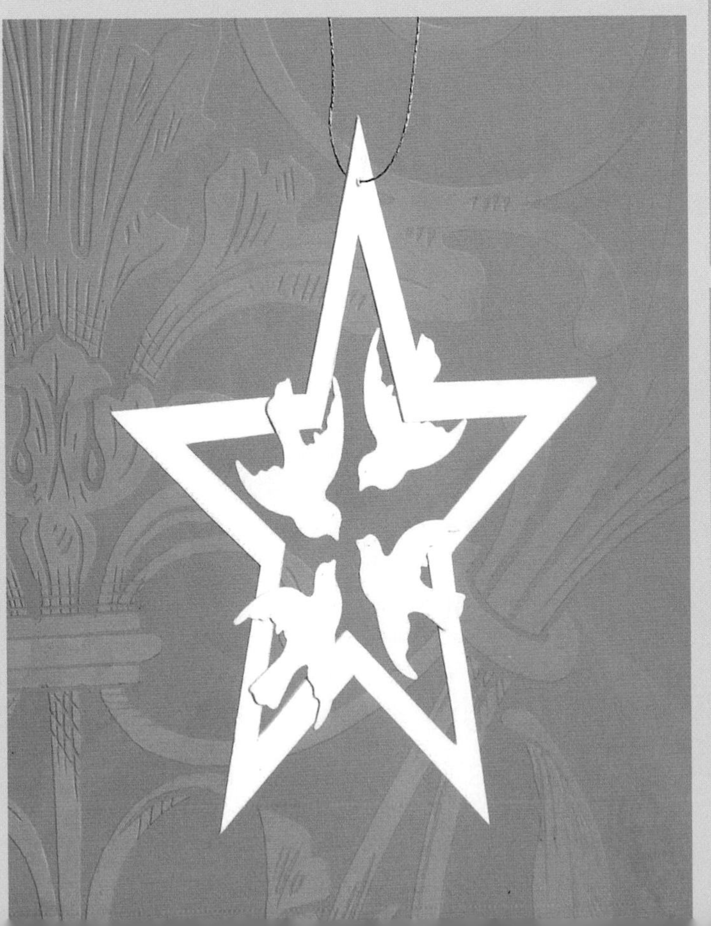

Pure white cardstock and paper-punched designs are layered to create **Elegant Paper Stars**, *left* and *above*. Each beautiful star is carefully cut, then embellished with papers punched from decorative punches and other trims. Instructions and patterns are on pages 154–156.

A metallic chenille stem and a little cookie cutter are all you need to make **Simple Star Gazers**, *opposite*. Get the whole family involved making these magical little stars. **Beaded Star Place Cards**, *above*, set the stage for a heavenly holiday table. Wires are curled and the bases are covered in golden beads. Instructions are on pages 155–157.

151

Simple Wire Stars, *above*, announce that the holidays are near. Made from different weights and types of wire, these stars are easily formed to poke into window boxes. Layered felt shapes make **Bright Felt Stars**, *opposite,* to hang on your Christmas tree or to use as a gift tag. Simply cut and layer the stars and then add a string of colorful beads. Instructions are on page 157.

Golden Table Runner

Shown on pages 146–147

WHAT YOU NEED

Tracing paper; pencil
1 yard yellow cotton fabric
¼ yard gold cotton fabric
½ yard fusible web
¾ yard fusible thin cotton batting
Gold metallic sewing thread
Gold metallic embroidery floss
Matching sewing thread
Point turner

WHAT YOU DO

1. Enlarge and trace or copy star patterns onto paper and cut out. With right sides of yellow fabric together and using Star 1, cut two shapes for each star to make 12 total finished stars. Cut 12 stars from batting using Star 2. Trace 12 stars, using Star 3, onto fusible webbing paper. Fuse webbing to wrong side of gold fabric and cut out shapes. Fuse batting to wrong side of one yellow fabric star shape from each pair.

2. With right sides together, stitch ¼-inch seam line around outside edges of star, leaving an opening on one long side for turning. Clip inside points and trim outside points. Turn stars right side out and press flat, pressing seam allowance open for turning. With matching sewing thread, edge stitch close to pressed edges, stitching opening closed at the same time.

3. Fuse gold star to centers of larger yellow stars. Using gold metallic sewing thread machine sew decorative stitches around gold stars, through all layers. Using 2 strands gold metallic embroidery thread, sew straight stitches through center of each gold star to make star centerlines.

4. Lay out 12 stars in desired arrangement desired, having points or some edges touching. Tack the points together using matching sewing thread. Joining stitches can be sewn by hand or by machine, using a bar tack or button sewing stitch.

Elegant Paper Stars

Shown on pages 148–149

WHAT YOU NEED

Tracing paper or copier; pencil
White cardstock
Self-healing cutting mat
ExActo knife; metal edge ruler
White crafts glue
Toothpicks
Sewing needle or tac pin
Snowflake and dove paper punches
1⁄32-inch hole punch
Fine metallic thread for hanger threads
Assorted holiday sequins
Soft white eraser; scissors
½-inch embossed sequins
¼-inch star sequins

WHAT YOU DO

1. Trace or copy desired pattern, *opposite*, and on *page 156*, onto cardstock lightly with pencil.

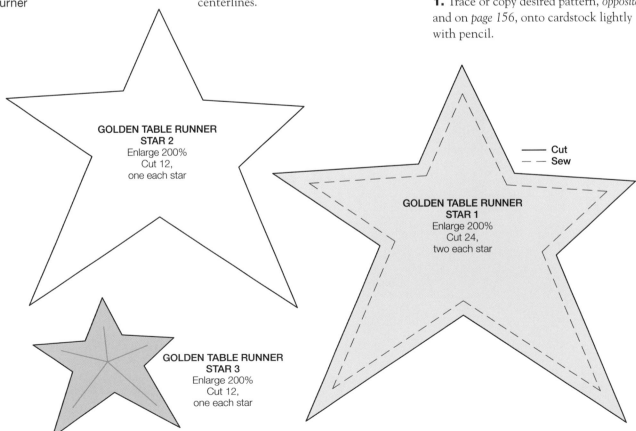

GOLDEN TABLE RUNNER
STAR 2
Enlarge 200%
Cut 12,
one each star

GOLDEN TABLE RUNNER
STAR 3
Enlarge 200%
Cut 12,
one each star

GOLDEN TABLE RUNNER
STAR 1
Enlarge 200%
Cut 24,
two each star

—— Cut
- - - Sew

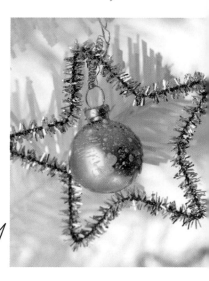

place them so a wing or tail is in front or behind star for 3-dimensional viewing. On some, gluing a cutout on front and back will achieve this, especially where sequins are used.

6. Cut length of metallic thread for hanging, punch hole, and insert through hole and knot.

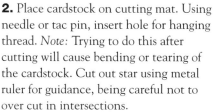

2. Place cardstock on cutting mat. Using needle or tac pin, insert hole for hanging thread. *Note:* Trying to do this after cutting will cause bending or tearing of the cardstock. Cut out star using metal ruler for guidance, being careful not to over cut in intersections.

3. For 5-point star with dove inside dove cutout, punch dove out after cutting out the star shape, then cut out "V" shapes at the tips of the star. Then at contact points glue (using tiny drops of glue on a point of a toothpick) the dove cutout perpendicular to the opening. This may need to be propped to dry.

4. For each star, cut out the star shape and then do all the interior cuts. Carefully erase any remaining pencils marks.

5. Glue with tiny drops of glue any snowflake/dove/sequins to designated places on the stars. On 5-point star with 4 doves, attach only 4 dove cutouts but

Simple Star Gazers
Shown on page 150

WHAT YOU NEED FOR ONE ORNAMENT
Star-shape cookie cutter
Chenille stem in metallic gold or silver
Small ornament; fine thread
Narrow ribbon or fine cording

WHAT YOU DO

1. Lay the cookie cutter on the table. Form the chenille stem around the cutter, pressing into the shape. Twist the top together. Reform if necessary. Add ribbon or cording to hang.

2. If desired, use fine thread to tie a small ornament inside the star area.

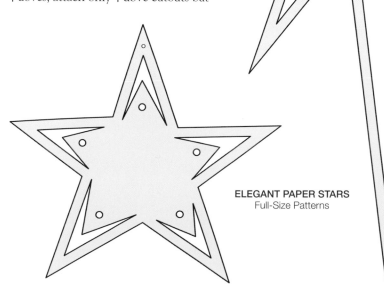

ELEGANT PAPER STARS
Full-Size Patterns

ELEGANT PAPER STARS
Full-Size Patterns

Beaded Star Place Cards

Shown on page 151

WHAT YOU NEED

Assorted wood star shapes
   (1⅛- to 3⅜-inch sizes)
Gold spray paint
Crafts glue
Classy glass beads variety
Gold fairy dust glitter
20-gauge brass wire
Wire cutter
Clear acrylic gloss spray
Hot-glue gun; glue sticks

WHAT YOU DO

1. Spray all wood star shapes with gold spray paint and let dry. Largest star shapes are used for a flat base and are painted only. Spread crafts glue on one side of 2 medium-size wood stars to be used for holding wires and sprinkle on glass beads or glitter. Let dry. Spray clear acrylic finish over all shapes to seal and protect finish.
2. Cut wire in 14-inch lengths. Shape wire into coils or star shapes, bending or looping as desired. Make an angle bend at the end of each wire. Sandwich wire between 2 glittered star shapes and hot glue together. Hot-glue glittered stars with wires to largest gold star shapes and hold firmly until dry. Place card between wires.

Simple Wire Stars

Shown on page 152

WHAT YOU NEED

Large piece of paper; pencil
Wire in various gauges: 20-gauge,
   18-gauge, and 16-gauge
Wire cutters

WHAT YOU DO

Decide on the size of the stars that fit best in the chosen windowbox. To help to estimate the size, use a pencil to draw simple star shapes on the paper. Use these drawings to form the wire star shapes leaving a long piece of wire at the bottom for poking into the windowbox. Form stars and poke into a windowbox. Add greenery. Add other lights to the box if desired.

Bright Felt Stars

Shown on page 153

WHAT YOU NEED

Tracing paper or copier; pencil
Three colors of felt; crafts glue
Scissors; inking shears
Gold sewing thread; needle
Beads in assorted sizes

WHAT YOU DO

1. Trace or copy patterns, *below.* Draw around patterns onto desired colors of felt and cut out using regular or pinking shears. Layer the stars from the largest to the smallest and glue together.
2. Thread the needle with gold sewing thread and string beads in desired order. Loop through the bottom bead and back up through the beads to secure. Sew to the bottom of the star.
3. Rethread the needle with gold thread and sew through top point for a hanger.

FELT STARS
Full-Size Patterns

Tips for Felting Wool

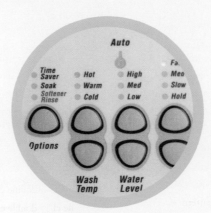

"Felting" wool fabric brings the fibers in the wool closer together and gives it a more compact look and feel. The texture becomes more irregular and interesting. Always choose 100% wool fabric to felt. Sweaters that are nearly 100% wool will work, but the fibers will not be as tight.

Sweaters that have less than 90% wool will not work well.

Place the wool inside an old pillowcase to prevent any tiny fibers from washing out. Then wash the wool in very hot water with a little laundry detergent. Agitation of the wool loosens fibers and helps to

shrink the wool. Dry the wool in a hot dryer to shrink the maximum amount.

Press the wool with a press cloth if desired. Tightly felted wool does not ravel, and edges and seams can usually be left raw or unfinished similar to purchased felt.

All About Ribbon

All kinds of wonderful ribbons are available at crafts stores, fabric stores, scrapbook stores, and discount stores.

Ribbon can be purchased by the yard or by the roll. Buying on the roll is usually more economical. However, buying more-expensive ribbons by the yard offers the opportunity to choose these ribbons if just a little of the beautiful ribbon is needed.

Ribbon is made from a variety of fibers including satin, silk, cotton, or even paper. The style of the ribbon or how it is woven also varies. Some ribbon types include grosgrain ribbon, satin-faced ribbon, sheer-woven ribbon, metallic, and printed ribbon.

Some ribbon has a wired edge that gives it more body to hold a shape. Other ribbon has no wire in the edge and flows naturally. Each style of ribbon offers lovely results.

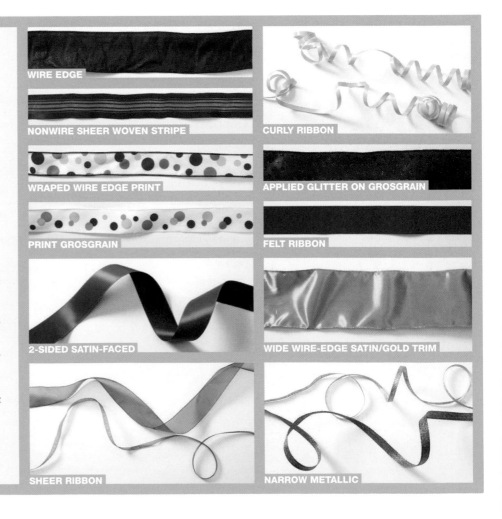

WIRE EDGE

NONWIRE SHEER WOVEN STRIPE

WRAPED WIRE EDGE PRINT

PRINT GROSGRAIN

2-SIDED SATIN-FACED

SHEER RIBBON

CURLY RIBBON

APPLIED GLITTER ON GROSGRAIN

FELT RIBBON

WIDE WIRE-EDGE SATIN/GOLD TRIM

NARROW METALLIC

Stitch Diagrams

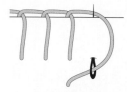

Blanket Stitch

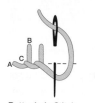

Buttonhole Stitch

Chain Stitch

Fern Stitch

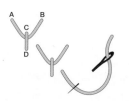

Fly Stitch

Lazy Daisy Stitch

Stem Stitch

Knitting Abbreviations

approx	approximately
beg	begin(ning)(s)
cn	cable needle
dec	decrease(s)(ing)
end	ending
est	established
inc	increase(s)(ing)
k or K	knit
p or P	purl
pat	pattern
pwise	as if to purl
rem	remain(s)(ing)
rep	repeat(s)(ing)
rev	reverse
RS	right side(s) of work
sl	slip
sm	slip marker
st(s)	stitch(es)
St st	stockinette stitch
tbl	through the back loop(s)
tog	together
WS	wrong side(s) of work
yo	yarn over
yon	yarn over needle
yrn	yarn around needle
[ ]	work step in brackets the number of times indicated
( )	work instructions within parentheses in the place directed and the number of times indicated
*	repeat the instructions following the single asterisk as directed

Crocheting Abbreviations

approx	approximately
beg	begin(ning)(s)
bet	between
ch	chain
ch-	refers to chain or space previously made
ch-sp	chain-space
cont	continue
dc	double crochet
dc cl	double crochet cluster
dec	decrease
end	ending
est	established
foll	follow(ing)(s)
hdc	half double crochet
inc	increase
lp(s)	loop(s)
pat	pattern
rem	remain(ing)(s)
rep	repeat
rnd(s)	round(s)
RS	right side
sc	single crochet
sl st	slip stitch
sp(s)	space(s)
st(s)	stitch(es)
tog	together
WS	wrong side
yo	yarn over
[ ]	work instructions within brackets as many times as directed
( )	work instructions within parentheses as many times as directed
*	repeat instructions following the single asterisk as directed
**	repeat instructions between asterisks as many times as directed, or repeat from a set of instructions

Sources

Hammond's Candies
hammondscandies.com

Hobby Lobby
hobbylobby.com

Michaels
michaels.com
1-800-michaels

Ribbon
craftopia.com
hancockfabrics.com
joannfabrics.com
jordanpapercrafts.com
mayarts.com
mjtrim.com
papermart.com
offray.com
midoriribbon.com
ribbonlady.com
ribbonshop.com

Paper/Scrapbooking Supplies
American Craft
americancrafts.com

Bazzill
bazzillbasics.com

Chipboard Letters:
Basic Grey Chipboard letters
basicgrey.com/r

Doodlebug
doodlebug.ws

EK Success
eksuccess.com

Ki Memories
kimemories.com

Making Memories
makingmemories.com

Mod Podge
plaidonline.com

My Mind's Eye
mymindseye.com

Provocraft
www.provocraft.com

QuicKutz
www.quickutz.com

Versamark Archival Ink
www.tsukineko.com

index